Rising To Greatness

Also, by Brian Hunter

The Hunter Equation
Secret Whisperings from God & The Universe

The Hunter Equation brings clarity and answers to the most complicated questions and mysteries of the Universe, God, and Humanity. Brian has successfully managed to reconcile science, spirituality, and religion, into one viable set of theories that make sense and explain how the Universe works.

A few of the topics covered include an explanation of God, living energy, the eternal human soul, the cycle of life, death, life after death, how psychic ability works, karma, destiny vs. free will, Angels, spirit guides, how prayer works, humans, aliens, and the future of humanity.

Where the Law of Attraction is incomplete and left many people disappointed with their results, Brian Hunter introduces his own Universal equation that more accurately reflects the reality and truth of the Universe. Brian's more realistic and commonsense alternative to the Law of Attraction is more useful and effective in achieving desired results. This is a must-read for people of all ages and beliefs.
There is something in this book for everyone.

Rising To Greatness

Fixing Your Life

By

Brian Hunter

Published by

Rainbow Wisdom

Ireland

ABOUT THE AUTHOR

Brian Hunter is a well-known American psychic counselor, Life Coach, and author based in Los Angeles, California. Brian grew up highly intuitive, but after a major paranormal event, his abilities increased, and he shortly thereafter became a professional psychic. Brian has been a member of Best American Psychics and was listed as one of the top 50 psychics in the world. Brian has worked with people from all over the world, including celebrities and captains of industry. Brian was an original cast member of the TV series pilot "Missing Peace," in which psychics worked with detectives to solve cold cases. He has also worked as an actor in Hollywood, featured in various movie and TV productions unrelated to his psychic work. Brian is the author of the groundbreaking book *The Hunter Equation*, which is changing how people view Spirituality, the Universe, and how the Law of Attraction works and does not work. Brian currently works with clients to transform their lives, has done psychic readings, and work as a psychic Medium, Healer, and Energy worker. Brian is available for lectures, and private and public events.

www.thehunterequation.com

DEDICATION

This book is dedicated to you. Dedicated to all those who have the courage to Rise To Greatness.

Also dedicated to all those open and inquisitive enough, who read *The Hunter Equation* to expand their awakening, rather than remaining closed with judgment.

CONTENTS

Chapter One

Greatness

Many of us are to a smaller or larger degree broken in some way. Most of us can relate to those moments of frustration, discouragement, sadness, hopelessness, and despair. Some of us more than others have suffered in varying degrees. Disappointment, losses, failures, near misses, rejections, and a feeling of not being good enough, are common and can really get us down.

Some of us have suffered painful losses and still grieve. Some have been betrayed by the ones we trusted most. Some of us worked tirelessly, only to see our work turn into nothing in the end. Some have lost their careers and their family homes. Some have lost their marriages and relationships. Some lost family members or children, through divorce, bad circumstances, or even worse. Others feel they have lost their dignity and self-respect. Worst of all, some have lost hope.

Whatever your tragedy, loss, or struggle, I grieve with you. I know it is difficult. I have been there. I have suffered multiple losses that stole all of my hope, humanity, dignity, and essentially my life. I have cried until there were no more tears left, and I have been at the point of suicide. I understand how bad and hopeless it can feel. Most of us have some pain deep inside us from something. Some hide their pain, some bury it in bad habits, and others display it openly as a hot mess.

So, let us agree on one thing. We have all been hurt at some point in some way. That pain inflicted damage upon us. It might have made us crawl deep inside ourselves. Maybe we stopped taking risks. Maybe we gave up on our dreams. Maybe we simply gave up, period. Or maybe we just stopped living and are a walking dead. What it most certainly did, was beat us down and discourage us. This makes us feel like less of a person. With our spirit damaged, broken, or missing, we start to crawl through life as if we have already died. We cease living and are simply just surviving. We live in quiet desperation. We live in pain. We live thinking our life will never be more than what it is today.

I do not want you to live in that pain with those limitations. I want to help you. I want to help lift you up. I love you, and you deserve more. You deserve a chance to live up to your full potential. You deserve a second chance, a third chance, and perhaps some of you need even more than that (smile). But you deserve another chance. You deserve to be happy. You deserve to live life to the fullest.

A new day is dawning. The pain, struggles, and limitations of the past need to be wiped aside. You need to say enough is enough. It is time to rise up out of the ashes like a phoenix. It is time to rise to greatness.

True, I cannot wave a magic wand and make everything all perfect. I cannot promise that just reading this book will fix everything. But what I can do is take your hand and bring you on a journey of self-discovery, self-improvement, and transformation. I can guide you through various steps to greatness. I can light a pathway for you to walk.

You need to choose whether or not to walk down the path. It is your journey, not mine. But if you have had enough of the pain, struggle, limitations, depression, and discouragement that your past or present situation may have brought you, then I urge you to take my hand and walk down the path. I will show you the way. This is your time. This is your time to be Rising To Greatness.

But first, what is "greatness" anyway? Does greatness mean great wealth, a big house, being rich and famous, or inventing the next great thing? No. For our purposes here, I am going to define "greatness" as reaching your base level of potential for success, happiness, inner peace, and fulfillment. Reaching greatness means being a great person full of deep moral character. Reaching greatness means having self-respect, dignity, and having earned the respect of others. Greatness means reaching a level that makes you proud to be you. Reaching greatness means you feel good about yourself, who you are, and what you are doing. Reaching greatness means you love who you are.

Obviously, this is all relative and is going to be different for each person. Some of you will be rising up out of the ashes of total destruction. Others of you already feel you are in a great place in life, but you aspire to much greater heights. All of you can reach your goals. Thus, those of you who feel I am being overly dramatic and depressing because your lives are already pretty good, or you are already considered "successful," please know there is plenty in this book to make you even greater and more awesome than you already are. You will be a far more powerful Jedi when we are done, I assure you. But I will also still be speaking to those who need to be lifted up from underneath piles of rubble that life may have thrown onto them.

Regardless of where each of you are starting out in this process, the term of rising to greatness applies equally, and you are all capable of rising to the highest levels of greatness that life has to offer.

I have learned from experience that people are capable of amazing things if they are given the chance, the skills, and the tools. I will go under the assumption that you already possess the desire and character necessary to take on this challenge of rising to greater heights. So what

I will be focusing on is offering all of the skills, knowledge, and tools necessary for you to achieve success on this adventure.

For the most part, humans are dumped into this world with no warning, little preparation, and no experience. You are left to struggle on your own and figure things out the hard way. You were not issued an owners-manual or instruction book. I am about to give you that instruction book now. There are indeed certain traits and skills that enable humans to have a better chance of success and happiness. We will be covering these various traits and skills so that you may pick them up, incorporate them into your "self," and use them to your fullest advantage.

Part of this process we are embarking on is to give you all possible advantages to maximize your chances of success and reaching your highest potential. I want to give you an edge over everyone else. Please accept this opportunity to re-boot your life, re-discover yourself, re-invent yourself, and find yourself all over again. I have written all of this for you and have done it with love. My dream for you is that you can release your pain and limitations, take on all of these skills you are about to learn, and start Rising To Greatness. I believe in you, and I know you can do it. So now what do you say we get started...

Chapter Two
Wiping The Slate Clean

I know I just got you all excited to start on your journey of transformation and learning all the life skills I mentioned, but if you are currently a hot mess, you have some important business to take care of before you get started. First, you need to take out the garbage and wipe the slate clean. You are not going to build a castle on a foundation covered with debris from previous damage. You need to clear out all the debris so that you have a nice clean foundation with upon which to build. Don't worry, I will help you.

You have likely sustained various amounts of damage thus far in your life. This damage will have affected how you look at life, and how you behave. It may have made you sad, angry, resentful, a bit timid, all out scared, depressed, or discouraged. The damage and trauma may have even caused you to lose hope.

All of this damage and trauma littering your mind, body, heart, and soul is garbage that needs to be thrown out. Like with any renovation project, we first have to rip out the bad stuff, and clean out the entire area, before we can start building the new stuff.

TAKE INVENTORY

What I would urge you to do is write down your major items of garbage. You want to write down anything that hurts you or holds you back. Write down anything that makes you feel bad such as mistakes, failures, losses, life traumas, betrayals, and scarring or damaging moments. Write them all down. This will be your one big pile of junk.

Then I want you to divide all this junk into two piles. One pile is all the items that you did to yourself, such as mistakes and bad choices. The second pile is all the items that others did to you, or things that happened to you which were outside your control.

Let us look at the first pile of items that you felt were things of your own doing. Everyone makes mistakes. Making decisions, taking risks, trying things, taking action, are all things we must do in order to have a full life. Sometimes those choices, actions, and risks, do not pay off and do not work out well. Sometimes we make mistakes out of weakness, ignorance, or bad luck. Sometimes our train becomes derailed and we are totally off the tracks for a period of time. Life happens. Humans are not perfect. You are not perfect, and those who have harmed you are not perfect.

FORGIVE YOURSELF

Sort through the first pile of junk, which are all the items you did to yourself through your own mistakes and bad choices. Forgiving oneself is often one of the most difficult things a person can do. In my opinion, it is far more difficult than forgiving others. Sometimes people even find it impossible to forgive themselves.

In my years counseling people, I have found one of the major causes of addiction to be unhappiness and depression as a result of a person engaging in self-hate, carrying guilt, or having shame over their past.

Whether it is failed relationships, business/career failures, or major wrong turns in life, we can end up beating ourselves up over it for years. "Why was I so stupid?" "What if I had not been so lazy?" "Why did I do this?" "Why did I do that?" "Why was I so weak?" "Why was I so blind?" "What was wrong with me?" "Why was I so slow?" "Why did one mistake ruin my life?" We can go on and on. Everyone can relate to one or more of the phrases above.

Beating ourselves up over the past is a form of self-abuse. It would be the same if some outside person kept calling you a loser or stupid over and over every day. How would that make you feel? How would that affect your psyche? It would make you feel like a loser and be debilitating to the point where you would not be able to succeed effectively. We would consider the person saying these things to you as abusive and toxic. Yet, we do this to ourselves all the time. We constantly abuse ourselves over past events. We become abusive and toxic to ourselves.

Forgiving ourselves is how we stop being abusive and toxic to ourselves. We have to stop right here and do this before we proceed. You cannot move forward in this process and succeed if you continue to be abusive and toxic toward yourself. It has to end today.

So here is how we are going to do this. We are dividing you into two lives. The person you were, and the person you are becoming now.

The person you WERE was the person who made the mistakes. That person is in the past. The person you are becoming now is the person you are presently as you read this. The line is drawn.

The person you are now has not made any mistakes. Unless your food is burning on the stove right now as you read this, no mistakes have been made yet for you to beat yourself up over. So be the person you are NOW. It's okay; you can start anew now. If you needed this second, third, fifteenth or more chance, I am giving it to you now. You deserve another chance. Everyone deserves another chance at life. I am urging you to take it. It is a gift from the Universe. It is a gift to yourself. You get to start new again now.

So, you are starting new NOW.

Okay, so now we are looking backwards at the person you WERE. That person made some mistakes and bad choices. It happens. Humans are not perfect. Nobody is perfect. But that person also did some good things as well. That person deserves forgiveness. Acknowledge the mistakes made. Face them. Admit to them. But remember, they are in the past and you are no longer that person. You are a new person now. You have to let it go. Let it go.

Again. You have to let it go. Seriously. Let it go. I will tell you this. If you do not let it go, you will poison yourself to death with toxin. You either continue making yourself suffer and continue suffering in your same life of before, or you let it go and move forward with all of us now into your new life.

I told you at the beginning I was offering you my hand to help you up. Do you want to take my hand and get up? Or do you want to stay down in the mud? Come on now. Take my hand. It is time to move forward. Let it go. Leave it behind.

Breathe it out. Look up. Let it all go. Take a bathroom break if you need it. Get something to drink if you need it. Stick your head outside for just a moment. Smell the air. Look at the sun. Look at a picture of your favorite person or family member. Take a moment. And then let the past go. Just let the past go.

You have forgiven yourself because you have now moved on. That was then; this is now. NOW you are a new person. Now you are a person who has chosen to move forward. In order to move forward, you had to leave the past behind. You had to forgive yourself.

From now on, you are no longer allowed to abuse yourself. We will teach you how to love yourself. But okay, let us not get ahead of ourselves. For now, you can no longer abuse yourself. Whenever you feel any self-hate, guilt, disgust, or disappointment in yourself, you need to stop. You need to take a moment and remember what we just did. You may need to let it go again. You cannot move forward unless you let it go. So, let it go.

I forgive you. I love you. The Universe loves you. I want you to have another chance at life. I want you to have a better life. So, if I care enough about you to give this to you, then you must care enough about yourself to offer yourself the same consideration and opportunity.

I am very happy for you that you have chosen to give yourself a chance at a better life. Today you have given yourself an amazing gift. You have also proven to yourself that you love yourself enough to do this. It is not easy to just forgive and let go. But you deserve it and you must do it to find happiness.

Congratulations on the new you! Since this is new, you might be a bit fragile. So be careful and caring about yourself, who you engage with, and what you engage in, until you become more solid in your new life. When we pour new concrete, it will end up being solid and almost indestructible, but while it is wet and drying, we have to stay off it and protect it. So be easy on yourself. But now you are ready for the next step.

DEALING WITH OTHERS

Now that you have dealt with yourself and forgiven yourself, it is time to deal with others. It is time to deal with all that junk in that second pile. Are there people you feel you need to apologize to for something? Are there people you feel you need to break off contact with? Do you have unfinished business with others? This is the time to take care of all this.

If in forgiving yourself you felt a need to apologize to others, this is the time to do that. Go to that person or persons (or write them) and face up to what you did. Acknowledge it. Take responsibility. Tell them you realized it was wrong. Tell them you are sorry if you hurt them. Tell them you are currently working on yourself and are moving forward as a better person.

Then leave it behind you. You are done with it. The other person does not need to acknowledge you on this. The other person does not need to forgive you. The other person does not need to say or do anything. The other person does not, and will not, control your ability to move forward as a new person in this process. Nothing they say can stop you. Even if they do not accept your apology, it does not matter. The only requirement here is that you faced up to what you did, owned it, and apologized. That's it. Then you get to move on and move forward in this process.

The next piece of this is detaching from those people in your life who have been toxic, abusive, or harmful to you. You have already done the hard work of stopping the abuse toward yourself. Now you have to stop the abuse others have inflicted upon you. So, if there are people who are abusive or toxic, you need to distance yourself from them now. Do not engage in drama to do this. Do it quietly. Do it humbly. But do it.

If you now have the self-respect to no longer abuse yourself, you also have the self-respect to no longer allow others to abuse you. So that ends today also. Even if you end up lonely, you must detach from any abusive toxic people. If those people are your family or co-workers, you need to separate as much as possible. Even if you cannot physically separate, you can mentally separate. You can, with your mind, choose to no longer let them into your psyche. You are no longer freely allowing mental abuse from yourself or from others.

STOPPING BAD HABITS & BAD BEHAVIOR

Up to this point, we have been focusing on the mental and emotional garbage and baggage. Now it is time to focus on the physical garbage and baggage. What bad habits do you have? Vices? Addictions? Poor behavior? Destructive behavior or activities?

I would have to write a totally separate book on ending addictions and bad behaviors. So, for our purposes here, I need you to take inventory of what bad habits you have. Acknowledge them. Then decide which ones you choose to change. A person does not have to stop all bad habits in order to proceed with this process. Sometimes, a person needs to go through the entire transformation process, and that is what leads them to stopping bad habits in the end. But with that said, the more bad habits you can reduce or stop now, the better this process will work for you. In other words, the more garbage you can remove now, the better your renovation results will be in the end.

So, identify what bad habits you have and begin to fix them. Simply stop or modify any bad habits or bad behaviors. We already decided to stop all mental abuse. Now it is time to stop all physical abuse, if you will allow it. If you have been thinking about stopping any bad habits lately, THIS is the perfect time to do it. Start now. After all, you are starting a new life now. So, go BIG!

DIET & EXERCISE

Along with stopping bad habits, it is time to improve your diet and exercise. I am not trying to turn you into an Olympic athlete, or have you eating nothing but lettuce. That is not the point of this. What I am trying to do is get your new slate as clean as possible. Part of that is improving your physical health. A person in poor health, or who eats a poor diet, often feels like crap. So, if you feel tired or unmotivated, part of it will be your health. By modifying or starting your diet and exercise program, you can improve that, even if slightly.

This book is not about diet and exercise. That is another entirely different book I would have to write. Oh my, I have a pile of books I have to write all of a sudden. But for now, let's just say we need to improve your diet and exercise.

Here is my strategy on diet and exercise. Start small. Take baby steps. Never stop. As far as exercise, this might mean just going outside and walking around the block each day. It might only take you ten minutes. But do it. Then you can extend the distance and time when you are ready. How far and how long does not matter at first. All that matters, is that you do SOMETHING. So, feel free to set the bar low at first. That's the good news. That bad news is that you actually have to DO IT. So set something that you know you can easily handle every day or every other day. Then you can increase it slightly when you feel ready. Finally, once you start, you cannot stop. This will now become part of your permanent lifestyle. So, start slow, take baby steps, but STICK WITH IT.

Same with diet. You do not need to go from McDonalds to lettuce in a day. Start by just eliminating one or two things. No more soda. Or no more desert. Then work your way down from there. Give up something you know you can handle giving up. Then give up something else when ready. NEVER LOOK BACK. So, it is the same strategy for both diet and exercise.

The whole point is to clean your slate physically and health-wise, as well as mentally, and your life in general. When we started this chapter, you were a hot mess. You were abusive to yourself mentally and physically. You also received abuse from others. You were surrounded by garbage. You were wallowing in your own garbage and stuck there.

Now look at you. We have cleansed you. You are clean. You are fresh. You are in a new life. Now that you have wiped your slate clean, the healing and building can begin.

Chapter Three
Developing A Sense Of Self

You had an old structure that was no longer working for you. You tore out the old parts you no longer wanted. You removed all the demolition debris. You have taken out the garbage, swept away the dirt, and wiped the slate clean. You have let go of the past and moved on. You have started your new life as the new person you are presently becoming. We now have a good, clean, solid foundation to build upon. So, let's build!

After ensuring you have a solid clean foundation, the next step in construction is to put up the framing. The framing is the basic skeletal structure. The framing is what everything else will be built upon and around. Not only is the framing the basic structure, but it is the support that will keep the structure standing, and it is the design that determines how the finished product will appear and operate.

In this case, your basic framing structure is called your "sense of self". What is a Sense Of Self you ask? Your sense of self is your self-identity. It is knowing who you are, what you are, what you stand for, what you consist of, what you want, and what you don't want. Essentially, your sense of self is knowing who you are fully, acknowledging it, accepting it, and owning it. Your sense of self is the skeletal super structure we are building on your foundation.

Why is having a sense of self important? You have to have a sense of self, so you know who you are. If you don't know who you are, you will always feel lost, unsure of yourself, unclear of your goals and priorities, and unmotivated because you have no clear objective or picture of yourself. People with no sense of self wander aimlessly and are never sure what they want, where they should be, who they should be with, or what they stand for. They tend to just live each day without living. It would be analogous to trying to build a house without blueprints. What a mess.

So, let's make sure you have a clear design and a solid structure to further build upon. Let's make sure the design is what you want, and the structure has all the rooms you desire. Let's make sure we build something you will be happy with and proud of in the end.

DEFINE YOURSELF

First thing you need to do is clearly define yourself. You need to see who and what you are now. Then identify any changes you want to make to your structure before we do any further building. This is where you might want to have a pencil and paper handy to take notes.

Part of what we will be doing is giving you absolute CLARITY on yourself. To do this, we have to look at the same thing from more than one angle. If you are going to buy a car, you don't just look at the front. Oh, how pretty and shiny, it's just been washed. I'll buy it! NO! You look at the front, sides, back, inside, under the hood, inside the trunk, and under the chassis. You look at the clean, the nice, as well as the dirty and worn, right? So that is what we are going to do now with YOU.

First, write a very brief paragraph or sentence describing yourself as how you were in the past before you cleaned your slate. Secondly, do the same thing describing how you see yourself NOW, after the slate cleaning. Thirdly, do the same describing how you ultimately would like to be seen in the future. Finally, write a description of how you think others see you.

You should have four descriptions. Examine them. Notice the differences. Particularly, notice the difference between how you were before vs. how you are now. See the clarity on how you see yourself now. Then discard the description of how you used to be, shoving it to the side. That is ancient history at this point.

Next, examine the differences between how you see yourself now vs. how you feel others see you. Notice any differences. Gain clarity on the realization that how others see you is not really relevant. So, whether others see you in a more positive light, or more negative light, realize how others see you is immaterial. Discard it to the side. It's not relevant. Others do not define you.

Finally, examine the differences between how you see yourself now vs. how you would like to see yourself in the future. Then combine the two descriptions into one. Now you should have one description that is a combination of how you see yourself now, and how you would like to see yourself in the future. This is your new current description of yourself or working definition. This is the basic structure or the blueprints for your renovated structure. But now we need to further complete these with further detail.

TAKE INVENTORY

Take inventory of yourself. This is like making a list of all the building materials you already have available at your building site. We need to

23

know what you already have vs. what you will need to go get in order to finish your structure. More lists...

Write a list of your attributes. This is an honest list based upon your final combined description of yourself. For example, you might write down: Educated, Street-smart, Intelligent, Friendly, Shy, Lazy, Tired, Energetic, Psychic, Skilled at electronics, Good Listener, Athletic, Non-athletic, Generous, Careful, Care-free, etc, etc. Notice this is meant to be a realistic balanced list of all attributes, regardless of whether you view them as good or bad. This is not about fluffing up your ego or making yourself feel like a loser. This is about honestly taking inventory of what you have. If you do it correctly, it will have both good and bad things on the list. You can also add things to the list as you think of them going forward.

Next, you should make a list of your STRENGTHS and WEAKNESSES. Two separate lists. You can use some of the items from your ATTRIBUTES LIST to get started. But then try to add more items. The strengths and weaknesses lists are meant to be a critical close-up view of the attributes. Under weaknesses, write down all the things you see as weaknesses about yourself, and all the things that bug you about yourself. Under strengths, be sure to give yourself full credit for the things you are actually good at and you consider to be your positive points.

At this point, you should have three inventory lists: Attributes List, Strengths, and Weaknesses. First, examine your Attributes List. When you look at this list, it should give you the feeling of "This is who I am." Look at it. Look at it again. OWN IT. That's you. How does it make you feel? Do you feel good? Do you feel bad? Are you comfortable with it? This is all the "stuff" you chose to keep during our cleaning out phase. So, this is now a second chance to throw out anything you realize you don't want or don't need. Throw it out. Look over this list and throw things out until you feel comfortable with the list. The list is who you are. So, work on this list until you are comfortable with who you are. This is really where you have to own your own baggage. Know what you have. Face up to it. Own it.

Acknowledge it. Feel comfortable with it. It's your new structure. You need to feel comfortable with it before proceeding with your construction project.

Next, look at your strengths and weaknesses. OWN THEM. You have strengths. You will need them. You will use them. Be sure to take full advantage of them. Your strengths are your edge in this challenge we call life. Your weaknesses are your vulnerabilities. When looking at a weakness, you either need to eliminate it, minimize it, or accept it. All three options are acceptable, as long as you OWN IT in the end. Strengths are who you are, and weaknesses are who you are. You have to know them, accept them, and own them.

Wow, at this point you are really getting to know yourself. The good, the bad, and the ugly. Or for all you "positivity people" out there, we'll call it the beautiful and the wonderful. It's all you. It is like taking a good long stare at yourself in the mirror. Sometimes we like what we see, and other times we do not. But we need to know what we look like and own it.

Believe it or not, we are not done yet. So take a break if you need it. Sort of an energy detach, reset, then reattach. Now we will move forward.

MORAL STANDARDS

Let's now examine your Moral Standards. This is not so much how your structure will be constructed, but it is about how your structure will operate and function. Moral standards are a very personal thing. I cannot tell you what to believe in or how to conduct yourself. But you need to get clarity on these things in order to have a clear sense of self.

So take a moment and consider what your Moral Standards will be. When considering this, you may first consider what they used to be in the past. Consider how you want to be DIFFERENT from how you used to be. But also consider how you want to remain the same.

Additionally, consider what changes you wish to make.

The subject of Moral Standards can include your religious beliefs, spiritual beliefs, non-beliefs, as well as how honest you will be. For example, if you are in sales, you need to decide how far you will go to make the sale. Will you say ANYTHING to get the sale? Or will you exaggerate to a certain point? Or will you do neither? I am not here to judge you. For example, if you are trying to sell an old car, you will not sell it by saying "It's an old car that is a total pain and I think it will break and die any moment now". If you are that honest, you will never sell the car. But should you say, "This is the best car ever, and I have never had any problems with it"? Which would you say? Or do you say, "This is an old car and I have had some issues with it, but it's running fine right now"? You get the idea.

So you need to decide where on the honest scale you will be sitting. This will depend on your career partly. If you are a doctor, I pray you will sit more on the super honest side. But if you are a used car sales person, you are likely going to have to make some allowances (smirk). But decide how far you will go. How far you will exaggerate. Know your limits before you open your mouth.

The same applies when dealing with friends. Will you tell your friends whatever you want them to think, regardless of the truth? Or will you be 100% honest about everything with your friends, even if it is hurtful to yourself or them? What will it be? Where on the sliding scale will you sit?

Again, there are no wrong answers here and I am not judging you. But you must CLEARLY identify what your moral standards are, so that you can know yourself with absolute clarity. You need to know what your moral standards are, and OWN IT.

Are you comfortable with your moral standards? Do you cringe? Are you embarrassed? Are you proud? Are you confident? Go ahead and play with this idea, and shift ideas around until you are COMFORTABLE with your moral standards. Be comfortable, know them, and OWN IT.

LOVE YOURSELF

Now that you have more of a Sense Of Self, you need to love what you see and who you are. Do you? Or are you not sure? Let's take a closer look. More lists....

First, make a list of what you like about yourself, called LIKES. This is different from your attributes and strengths. The list of what you like about yourself should be things that make you FEEL good. So, these are not necessarily things you HAVE or ARE. These are things that give you a good FEELING about yourself. So, if you were writing glowing things about yourself, what would you say? What do you like about yourself?

Next, make a list of things you dislike about yourself, called DISLIKES. Again, this is more about how you FEEL. So yes, you may end up including things on your Weaknesses List. But you also may be adding more things that are not weaknesses but are just things you do not like about yourself. So, if you were writing about things you find annoying about yourself, what would you say? What do you dislike about yourself?

When finished, look at the Dislikes List. I am now giving you a THIRD opportunity to throw out more trash. So, look over this Dislike List carefully. Is there anything you dislike about yourself that you can just STOP doing, or CHANGE right now? If there are, and you want to, discard them now. Throw them out. If you are throwing them out, you can now ERASE them from your Dislike List. BUT, anything you ERASE, has to be something that is no longer a part of you. So be honest. Don't cheat. If it is still a part of you, keep it on the list. There are simply some things we do not like about ourselves that cannot be eliminated. It is part of who we are. We are not perfect. Nobody is perfect.

Now look at your Dislikes List in this new light. OWN IT. It's okay. We all have things we do not like. It's called real life. Have you any idea how much more powerful you are as a person, KNOWING what you do not like? Way more powerful than a person who lives in denial and will not even acknowledge anything they are too afraid to look at. So, facing up to, and owning our own dislikes actually makes us more powerful within ourselves. So, it's not all bad.

Now look at your Likes List. Is there anything you want to add? Did you forget some items? I know you did. I'm psychic, so this is how I know this. You left items off. Add them now. Be kind to yourself. Why would you be so cold to yourself? Think of it this way. Imagine a mean boss and imagine a nice boss. The mean boss only points out the bad and gives you no credit for anything good you do. The nice boss points out all the good things you have done, and then gives a suggestion or two on some corrections for improvement. Be the nice boss. Give yourself full credit for all the good you do, and all the good that you are. Be friendly to yourself. Be kind to yourself. Be loving to yourself.

BE loving. Thus, if you were to be LOVING to yourself, what would you add to the list? If you wanted to be encouraging to yourself, what would you add to the list? If you were trying to be motivational to yourself, what would you add to the list? Be generous to yourself. Add things even if they seem insignificant. Add things even if you think you only deserve partial credit.

Now step back. Look at yourself. You have a list of Dislikes. You did your best to throw out anything you could. You DID YOUR BEST. Give yourself credit for this. You also have a list of Likes. Once you lightened up a bit and started to show yourself some love, your Likes list grew. You have some good things about yourself you like.

Choose to be the nice boss. Acknowledge and own the Dislikes. Try to make corrections and improvements when possible. But focus on the Likes List. Give full credit for everything on it. Honor yourself. You deserve it. Life is not easy. Give yourself full credit. Encourage yourself. Motivate yourself. Be the nice boss. Show yourself some kindness. Show yourself understanding. Show yourself love.

IDENTIFY YOUR TRIBE

Knowing what our structure is and knowing what our blueprints consist of is not enough. Now we need to look at who our neighbors are. Directly put, what sort of people surround you? Who is your "Tribe"? Who is your family? You are probably sick of making lists by now, so I won't make you do it for this. But you should first consider who surrounds you. Think about who you work with, and who your blood related family is that you cannot escape from. Some of these people will be good, and some might be toxic. Identify them. Know who is good and who is toxic. We already talked about avoiding the toxic ones as much as possible.

But next, look at who your true tribe and family are. These are the people you truly resonate with. These are the people you truly trust and enjoy. You might be surprised to learn that how you see some of these people has changed. This is because you are a different person now. You may have changed a little, or you may have changed a lot. In either case, you need to re-evaluate all those surrounding you. You need to confirm who you can trust, who you cannot trust, who makes you a better person, and who drags you down. Sort through all those who surround you. Clearly identify those who truly resonate with the new person you are becoming. This is your tribe. With this in mind, you will want to spend more time with them, and less time with the others. This is an important part of the process because other people can have a large impact on how well you stick to your process of becoming greater than you were. You need to hang with those who will lift you up, rather than tear you down. Absolute clarity must be taken in identifying who your tribe is.

In extreme cases, some people have to actually disconnect from ALL people that used to surround them. Drug users trying to stay clean are a good example of this. So, you may need to disconnect from many people, or just a couple. You have to decide. You have to OWN IT.

SELF-VALIDATION

One of the major goals of developing a strong sense of self is that you will no longer need to search for validation outside yourself. You will no longer rely on other people to tell you if you are good or bad. You do not need others telling you if you are doing the right things or not. You do not need others telling you what is good about yourself or what is bad about yourself. You do not need others defining you and telling you who you are, or what you are. You do not need others patting you on the back for good things you have done.

Here is why this is important. Some people try to use outside validation as a way to manipulate you. Narcissists and sociopaths often offer you good and bad validations as a way of controlling you and manipulating you. They can make you feel bad or good to fit their own purposes and agendas. We will talk more in-depth about this later.

It is also important that you not be wasting your time and resources always looking around for other people to tell you if you are on the right track or not. You do not need to be wandering around aimlessly waiting for someone to say something nice.

One of the greatest freedoms you will ever have is the moment you no longer require any outside validation. You do not need outside validation. Why? Because you know who you are, what you are, what you want, where you want to be, and how you are going there. You know your attributes. You know your strengths and weakness. You know your likes and dislikes. You know yourself. So why do you need anyone else telling you who you are? You don't.

Know thyself. OWN IT. You have a strong Sense Of Self now. Thus, you are a more powerful person now. Congratulations on all your hard work so far!

Chapter Four
Eliminating Fear

We have cleaned out the old debris, you have a solid clean foundation, and you have built some well-designed "framing" of who you are. Now it is time to turn you into a warrior. The only way to do that is by eliminating fear. Fear is a human's biggest enemy. It is the enemy from within. Fear keeps us from doing things. Fear keeps us from reaching our desired potential. Fear keeps us paralyzed and stuck. Fear keeps us in discomfort and pain. Fear is evil. Fear has to go.

Our fears literally cripple us. They keep us from our dreams. They keep us from taking chances. They keep us from living our lives to the fullest. Fear keeps us from making necessary changes. Because of fear, we stay in toxic relationships, stay in horrible jobs, stay in destructive environments. Fear destroys lives and keeps us suffering in pain.

With all that said, is Fear good for ANYTHING? Yes. Fear can keep us from doing stupid things like touching a hot stove, cutting a limb off, falling off a cliff, or other physical harm. But that's about it. However, notice this type of fear is more related to physical and safety stimuli, and not to mental or emotional issues. This type of fear was meant to protect prehistoric humans from physical harm, which is why I felt I had to put in this caveat. But other than the primordial purpose of fear for safety's sake, mental and emotional fear is what we are focusing on.

Fear is one of the major nemeses of humanity. Not only does fear affect us directly by hurting our lives, but also fear causes us to hurt others. Fear very often leads to frustration and anger, which can lead to hate. Hate leads to irrational actions toward others. If I were Satan and I could only infect humans with one virus, I would infect them with fear. Fear is toxic for humans. It damages from the inside out, and from human to human. Again, fear is pretty much the definition of evil.

Even if you do everything we have talked about so far in this book, you will not get very far if fear is dominating your mind. Fear will stop you dead in your tracks and you will not get any further than here. So, we have a major hurdle to clear now, my friends. We must eliminate fear from your mind. In order to do this, we must first identify what you are afraid of. We must identify the fear, gain total clarity over it, isolate it, then eliminate it.

Imagine your life without fear. Imagine living with no fear. Imagine what you could accomplish. Imagine how much happier you would be. So, let's get started.

WHAT DO YOU FEAR?

Our first task it to try and identify what you fear. It is impossible for me to list every possible deep-seated fear of everyone. However, I will list many common fears below. Feel free to add your own fears to this list, even it means writing in your book.

-Fear of Dying
-Fear of Failure
-Fear of Success
-Fear of Rejection
-Fear of Embarrassment
-Fear of Harassment/Discrimination
-Fear of your Secrets Being Revealed
-Fear of Change
-Fear of Past Traumas
-Fear of Loved-Ones Dying
-Fear of Being Alone
-Fear of Abandonment
-Fear of Having No Value
-Fear of Other People
-Fear of Suffering & Pain
-Fear of Being Lost
-Fear of Being Helpless
-Fear of Aging
-Fear of Illness & Injury
-Fear of Dying Alone
-Fear of Living a Life of Quiet Desperation
-Fear of the Unknown

I am going to briefly examine each of these fears. Feel free to skip some if they are not relevant to you. I don't want to bore you. But it is important to fully engage with fears, as it is one of the most critical parts of this process we are engaged in, of Rising To Greatness.

FEAR OF DYING

The fear of dying is one of the most common fears. Why are you afraid of dying? You are not sure what will happen? You are afraid of the moment of death? You are afraid of where you might end up after dying? You are afraid because you will miss life and living? You are afraid because you won't be able to eat cookies anymore? What is it exactly? Ask yourself to pin it down. Why exactly are you afraid?

What I am asking you to do here is to face your fear head on. Look it straight in the eyes. Turn bright lights onto it. Study it. Touch it. Think about it. I call this "bathing in your fear." So, think about death. Think about what scares you the most. Face it: close-up. Then bathe in it by thinking about why it scares you so much.

Dying is something everyone does. Does that certainty scare you? Why? Is it because you have not done everything you wanted to do? Is it because you have unfinished business or things left unsaid? Identify exactly what bothers you most. Again, face it close up. Bathe in it. Get full clarity.

When we get closer to something and become more familiar with it, we become less afraid. This is why we have children come in close contact with different animals and insects. We do this to make them less afraid and less squeamish about animals and insects that they were naturally afraid of at first. So, bring yourself up close to death and touch it. Read about it. Think about it. Ask questions. Face it. Accept it.

Determine what it is about death that is most frightening to you. Then do the same process of getting close and examining it, touching, learning. If there are things you feel would be left undone or unsaid, then do them and say them. You need to become comfortable with yourself in case something happened to you tomorrow. This is a way of eliminating reasons to fear it. Process of elimination can be very helpful. So it may be a matter of making a list as to your reasons to fear death, then taking actions to eliminate some of the items. For the other items that cannot be easily eliminated, you want to educate and inform yourself as much as possible as to make yourself more familiar, and thus more comfortable, with the issue.

Look that alligator in the eyes. Touch it, wrestle in the mud with it, get dirty, and be totally familiar with it. Doing this tends to shed fear. Just watch your fingers! Because alligators bite. Just like dying means

34

death, it's a harsh thought. But it is what it is. To me death is a reminder to do as much as you can, while you can. Sometimes reminders are helpful and provide extra incentive. Use it as that. It's nothing to fear. It is something to be used as a reminder and incentive to act.

Becoming comfortable with death is a very personal thing, and what works for me might not work for you. So, you need to find what works for you. My point in this discussion is that you must face it, examine it close-up, touch it, bathe in it, and become familiar with it, so that you can become more comfortable with it. Don't fear it.

FEAR OF FAILURE

The next most common fear is the fear of failure. Humans fear failure so intensely that they will not even try to do something if there is any chance of failure. Fear of failure is likely the biggest block people have in trying things. Why do you fear failure? Mostly there are two reasons.

First, you are afraid of how you will feel if you fail. Are you afraid you will feel like a loser? Will you feel worthless? How will you feel? Are you really that afraid of a feeling? Are you so afraid of a feeling, that you will do nothing, and give up a chance at success and happiness?

Secondly, you are afraid of what others will say. Will other ridicule you? Pick on you? Will others call you a loser and laugh at you? Will others think you are a loser? Are you afraid of what others will say or think because what they say or think matters so much? Do you depend on other people for all of your validation and approval?

Are you going to let the risk of having a bad feeling for a while, along with the risk of others giving their worthless opinion, dictate your life and your future? Really?

Fear of failure is one of those fears where you have to lift up the board from the ground and look underneath it. You knew there would be nothing but bare ground, but your imagination never knows. In reality, you will see nothing but dirt. There is nothing there. Trying something and having it not work out, thus resulting in a hurt feeling for a period of time, is no excuse to not live your life to the fullest. Additionally, someone else's opinion or insults should not be the controlling factor in your life. Are you going to give other people such complete power over your life that their opinion or possible insult is enough to stop you from living your life to your fullest? Think about it.

Fear of failure. Face it. Look at it. It's nothing but dirt. Feel it. Touch it. Why are you scared of dirt? Screw what other people say if you have a setback. And if you are so worried about having bad feelings temporarily if you get a bad result on something, then we need to go shopping for some big boy or big girl panties for you. Because it's time to become bigger. You need to be able to handle some adversity and hurt feelings for a short time if you are going to survive on this earth.

Fear of failure is a huge dragon with no teeth and does not even breathe fire. It is like the big white fluffy Bumble in Rudolf. Big roar with no teeth. We are actually going to talk more about failure later in the book because it's so critical to deal with. But for now, let's accept that fear of failure needs to go away.

FEAR OF SUCCESS

Believe it or not, there are people who fear success. Why? Mostly, some fear success because they are afraid of either the responsibility it will bring, or they are afraid they will fail after they succeed. The saying goes, "the bigger they are, the harder they fall." This saying makes people afraid to become "big"(or successful).

You need to determine which reason causes you to fear success. If you are afraid of the responsibility success might bring, then you need to clearly identify what those responsibilities are that you fear so much.

List them. Then ask yourself what it is about those responsibilities that you fear. Identify them. Then you are able to develop solutions to eliminate those fears. Usually education, information, experience, and getting more familiar with something will take fear away. So, figure out which responsibilities you fear, and then become more familiar with those responsibilities so that you know you can do it, handle it, and take full ownership for it.

If the reason you fear success is because you are afraid you might later lose what you have gained, then you need to go back and read the section about "Fear of Failure". Being afraid of failing because you are successful is ridiculous even on its face. Please do not be that person.

FEAR OF REJECTION

Another of the major common fears is the fear of rejection. We are afraid we will put ourselves out on a limb just to be shot down by others, as if we are not good enough or don't have enough value. And I just said it, didn't I? We are afraid OTHERS will make us feel as if we are not good enough. We are afraid others will give us negative validation or take away our validation so that we are no longer validated.

Once again, you are putting your validation and value in someone else's hands for them to control and judge you. Why are you doing that? No outside person is qualified to determine your worth. In many cases, these people do not even know you. So why does their opinion and final judgment matter so much to you? Why does the possibility of some semi-stranger's rejection of you, cause you to not take actions or try things you want to do? Why are you giving other people so much power over you?

You need to go back to the prior chapter where we talk about your Sense of Self, resulting in you providing your own self-validation. You do not rely on the validations of others, especially strangers.

Realize that "rejection" is just someone else's opinion on

something. It is not your validation or value. It is only an opinion belonging to another person. Check to see you have those big boy or big girl panties on that we bought you earlier and accept the risk of feeling bad for a short time; but get over it and move on. Do not let a possible rejection control or stop you from living your life.

FEAR OF EMBARRASSMENT

Fear of embarrassment is similar to fear of rejection in that we fear we will look stupid in front of others. We are afraid we will do something stupid or get caught in a bad circumstance that will cause others to laugh at us. We are afraid people will laugh at us because we look stupid for some reason. That's the bottom line, right?

Here is the antidote for that: realize there will be times in life that you will look stupid and people will laugh at you. It's going to happen. It already has. We all got laughed at in school at some point unless you were one of the very few cool kids. Why fear something that is a fact of life? It is like being afraid of people seeing you eat, drink, or breathe. People do embarrassing things. People get caught in embarrassing situations. People get laughed at. It happens just like how we eat, drink, and breathe. It's common. Accept it. Please do not let some commonplace thing that happens to everyone stop you from living your life and doing what you need to do. Eventually you learn to laugh at yourself along with the others laughing at you.

FEAR OF HARASSMENT/DISCRIMINATION

Many people are kept from fully living because they are "different" in some way that makes them afraid of being picked out of the crowd and harassed or discriminated against. Maybe you look different, or have a disability, or have a different sexuality, gender identification, or some other feature that makes you "different." You fear if you have too high a profile that you will become a target.

Yes, it is very possible you could become a target of harassment or discrimination. I got picked on in school for being too skinny. I had it easy. But others face problems for being gay, transgender, overweight, too big, too small, having a limp, or having a speech impediment. There are many endless differences that can cause you to become a target for bullies.

Some humans are not very educated or evolved. Unfortunately, it's a fact of life. But again, are you going to let the words, validations, and judgments of others control your life? It is even worse when you take into consideration that the people targeting you are idiots. They do not even have the intelligence to render opinions that even matter. So, in this case we are dealing with opinions that do not even have any value. Even more reason to discard them out of hand. Accept the harassment and discrimination from others as "rain" that you just walk through and continue about your day. Bring your umbrella.

FEAR OF YOUR SECRETS REVEALED

I think we all have fears of our embarrassing secrets being revealed. Maybe we made mistakes and do not want anyone to know because we don't need it rubbed in our face. Or maybe we have secrets that happened, but they do not reflect how we are as a person today. We all have secrets and skeletons in our closet. We are afraid of taking any actions or risks that might result in those secrets coming out and being revealed.

How you deal with this is by making friends with your secrets and coming up with a backup plan in case they are revealed. Realize everyone has made mistakes and has secrets. Anyone who would reveal your secrets has embarrassing secrets of their own. Realize your secrets are part of your past.

Let's suppose they come out. Okay. Well, just tell it like it is. Say, "Yep", but then explain the circumstances and how horrible and embarrassed you feel about it, but how it has nothing to do with who you are in the present day. Or if it does have to do with your present day, be prepared to explain why you have to do what you are doing due to certain circumstances. Honesty is usually your best weapon here. It may be embarrassing, but the honesty usually explains it in a logical way that sets it aside for most people. Life goes on. Then you have one less secret and one less weapon for someone to use against you.

FEAR OF CHANGE

Fear of change is common, but one thing needs to be realized. EVERYTHING CHANGES. So being afraid of change is like being afraid of eating and drinking. I have found the best way to deal with the fear of change is to accept that change is an everyday reality. Instead of living every day fearing what will change, wake up each day and say, "I wonder what will change today". Then look for the change. From then on when you see change, you will say to yourself, "Ah, there it is." "I knew there would be a change today." You need to accept change as an expected event that will happen. Expect it, lean into it. Embrace it. You don't have to like it. But you must expect it and embrace the reality of dealing with it. Change is not to be feared. Change is to be expected.

FEAR OF PAST TRAUMAS

Some people have a fear of past traumas. If asked why they are afraid to do something, they will answer, "Because twenty years ago this bad thing happened to me." Humans naturally learn from past experiences. But sometimes that "programming" is counter-productive. If I pet a dog many years ago, and it bit me; that does not mean if I pet a dog today it will bite me. It means I had a bad experience in the past. People will literally be afraid to ever pet another dog again in their entire life because of that one past experience. Don't be that person.

Remember that past experiences do not always equal future results.

FEAR OF LOVED-ONES DYING

We all fear this. But we cannot let it stop us from living our lives and doing what we need to do. Perhaps go back and read the section on "Fear of Dying." But it is not lost upon me that many people don't fear their own death, but fear losing their partner or family member. However, this should not be a fear. This should be a reminder. This deep-seated natural fear should be a reminder to love and enjoy those close to you every day because we never know when someone might leave. Again, if this is an issue for you, then you need to spend more time wrestling "the alligator of death and dying" until you become more comfortable with it. You cannot let the fact that everyone dies stop you from living. How ironic for the fact of eventual death, paralyze you from living while you are alive.

FEAR OF BEING ALONE

The fear of being alone is quite common. This fear is the #1 reason why some people go from one toxic relationship to the next. Some people just cannot be alone. They would rather be with the wrong person than no person. If you are one of these people, you need to fix this, or you will be stuck right here at this point in the process. You cannot reach the end of full transformation to greatness if you insist on being in a toxic relationship with someone just because you are afraid to be alone.

Everyone with the fear of being alone should ask themselves one question. Why are you afraid of being alone? Do you not like yourself? Is the silence of being alone too deafening? Why are you uncomfortable just being by yourself?

If you are afraid of being alone, you need to make friends with yourself. You are never alone. I always say that I have "Me, Myself, and I." So, there are three of us at any given time. I know myself. I know what I like and what I don't like. I know how to amuse myself and what I enjoy. I sometimes talk to myself (when nobody is watching of course). Give me some music and good food, and I can even have a good time (the three of us). You seriously need to figure out what it is that you do not like about yourself. We will look at this more in the next chapter because it is so important.

FEAR OF ABANDONMENT

Fear of abandonment is similar to the fear of being alone, except for one difference. The fear of abandonment is more a fear of SUDDEN loneliness. This fear stems from depending on a person TOO MUCH, and then the fear of having them leave without warning. So, this fear is not just about being alone, but rather about depending on someone who is gone without warning and outside your control.

The antidote for this is to examine why you depend on any one person too much. This is a vulnerability. You should consider reducing the amount you depend on any one person. Taking pro-active action to ensure you can take care of yourself is a good way to deal with the fear of abandonment; since it reduces the consequences of the abandonment should it happen. Fears are often vulnerabilities that can be corrected, and this is one example of that. You need to put yourself in a position of always being able to become self-sufficient (physically & emotionally) should that be required.

FEAR OF HAVING NO VALUE

Many people at one time or another have a fear that they will be of no value to others, or the world in general. People ask, "What if I accomplish nothing?" Humans have a natural fear of living without purpose and leaving no legacy behind. People like to believe that they are contributing and adding value to lives, families, and the world.

The antidote for this is to have value. That is what this book is about. So keep reading. You have value now and will have even more value in the future.

FEAR OF OTHER PEOPLE

Many of us at one time or another are afraid of certain people. Maybe it's your boss, a co-worker, an ex, or someone else we have to deal with. This person is almost always toxic, although there are exceptions. Sometimes this person is actually someone you highly respect, but you feel intimated because you think they are out of your league.

There will be a chapter later on regarding toxic people. But with any person, you have to remember they also have weaknesses, secrets, vulnerabilities, fears, and they all put their pants on one leg at a time (although I've seen some women put pants on by jumping into both legs at once in an effort to squeeze into them). But at any rate, the fear of other people is usually because they are toxic or because you give them too much power. Do not give them all that power. Reduce them in size.

FEAR OF SUFFERING & PAIN

Humans naturally have a fear of anything that causes pain or discomfort. This is natural and even healthy if it helps keep us safe. What is not healthy is if this fear keeps you from living your life to the fullest.

You need to remember that we do not control everything. We do not have full control of our future. Anything can happen. The possibility of suffering and pain is always there and should be viewed as a possibility that will happen, regardless of what you do or don't do. So, there is no point in stopping yourself from living, since these things will happen regardless of what you do or don't do.

The thing to do is to have contingency plans and coping

mechanisms set up to deal the possible eventuality, should it happen to you. Being prepared is not just a Boy Scout motto. It is words to live by that can reduce fear.

FEAR OF BEING LOST

The fear of being lost can be literal or figurative. Some people literally have a fear of being lost driving, or as if in a maze. This often stems back from a fear of being separated from their parent as a child. The fear is a lack of coping mechanism for dealing with such an event. Thus, the antidote is to develop a contingency plan for such a possibility. Being prepared takes away fear.

Others have a fear of being figuratively lost in terms of not knowing what to do with themselves or their lives. If this is you, then simply keep reading this book. We are working on it.

FEAR OF BEING HELPLESS

We all fear being helpless. But the fear really stems from FEELING unprepared and BEING unprepared. So, the answer is to spend some time thinking about what your biggest fears or core issues are in regard to being helpless. Instead of fearing the monster in your closet and hiding under the covers, turn on all the lights, open up the closet, and thoroughly look inside the closet. Face your fears. Take action. Be prepared.

FEAR OF AGING

The fear of aging is usually a combination of the fear of dying and the fear you have not accomplished everything you wanted to accomplish. The first thing you need to do is focus in and determine what your exact fear or core issue is with your fear of aging. As with all problems and all our fears, you must first clearly identify and isolate the core problem. We have talked about fear of dying already. We have talked about fear of being helpless. Is your fear of aging related to a feeling that you have not accomplished what you wanted? Or is it that you feel you have not created anything of value yet? You need to have a good stare in the mirror and figure out exactly what it is. If you feel you have not done all you wanted, just keep reading this book because we are aiming to put you in a position to do whatever you have wanted to do in life.

FEAR OF ILLNESS & INJURY

It is normal for humans to have a fear of illness and injury. This is part of our protection mechanisms to keep ourselves healthy and safe. But when this fear becomes too powerful, it can paralyze us and cause us to lose sleep and devote precious resources to something we have little control over.

With that said, this is a very personalized subject. What I mean by that is we all have individual health and lifestyle issues. Someone who has a chronic disease will have different concerns than someone who does not. Someone who smokes will have different concerns than someone who does not. Thus, you need to evaluate your situation and actions needed based upon your individual health situation. This leads to the answer, which is to first see if there is anything you can do to prevent or limit any risks.

After you have mitigated risks within your control, you have to realize that you do not control everything. People get sick and people get injured. Accept it as part of the Universe. But you can mitigate your fears by being prepared and having contingency plans in place. This is another fear that fades once you look it square in the face, get more comfortable with it, and put plans and preparations in place.

FEAR OF DYING ALONE

The fear of dying alone is often related to the fear of dying. People are kind of scared to die, so they feel they need someone with them in order to not become as scared. So once again, I have to refer you above to the section about the fear of dying. But we need to look at one more thing when it comes to the fear of dying alone.

If you are to be totally honest with yourself, WHY or WHAT most scares you about dying alone? This is a good time to be honest with yourself. When we ask ourselves such questions, it gives us a chance to learn more about ourselves. Part of this process we are in, is to truly know ourselves and become friends with ourselves.

You need to be at peace with yourself. Why aren't you? Figure out why you don't feel at peace, and that will be your clue to the direction in which you should be looking.

FEAR OF LIVING IN QUIET DESPERATION

This fear is likely one of the reasons you are reading this book. You want to live life to the fullest and reach your full potential, right? So, keep reading.

FEAR OF THE UNKNOWN

The fear of the unknown is natural for humans. Humans have always feared what they do not understand. But humans are also curious creatures. So, let that curiosity help you overcome any fear of the unknown.

Ask yourself this: Why am I here on this Earth? Is it to just eat, sleep, and die? Or is it to experience and learn new things? The only way to experience and learn new things is to dive into the unknown. We have to walk into unknown territory in order to explore and find ourselves. Walking into the unknown is one of the most exciting things people do. Look at the unknown as a great adventure. It's living life. Do not be afraid to live life.

This look at fear was exhaustive. I have had enough of FEAR, and I am SO OVER IT. I presented it in this exhaustive way on purpose. I want you to be so annoyed and tired of fear that you are just DONE with it.

In general, the procedure for dealing with fear is to identify your fear, face it with clarity, examine it, feel it, touch it, wrestle it, become familiar with it, get comfortable with it, accept it, then dismiss it. Be over it. Do not relinquish any control or power over to fear. If you run into fear later on at any point, you may need to come back and read parts of this chapter again. Eliminating fear is critical for you becoming a warrior and Rising To Greatness.

Chapter Five
Living With Love

If I talk about "living with love," half of you will think I am being Mr. Positive Spiritual Guru, and will be excited to listen and learn how to be more positive and full of light. The other half of you are probably thinking I am being all "love and light" "woo-hoo" Namaste Blessings gag me with a spoon, and you are ready to throw up in your mouth because you are allergic to such talk, as I am most of the time. Both are wrong.

When I say, "living with love," I don't mean you have to love everybody and everything. That is not realistic. We do not love everyone. In fact, there are lots of people we do not like at all and will never like. We don't always feel love and happiness for everyone and everything. Despite what some of the motivational guru books say, it is not humanly practical to be 100% positive all the time.

What I mean by Living With Love, is to take difficult unhappy life situations, as well as people, and deal with them from the perspective of love. By Living With Love, I also mean that you need to treat yourself with love. So there is living with love on the inside, and living with love on the outside. Let's talk about the inside first.

LIVING WITH LOVE TOWARD YOURSELF

What does "living with love toward yourself" mean? Let's start to answer that by first asking how you currently treat yourself. How do you currently think of yourself? Do you like yourself? Do you respect yourself? Do you love yourself? We talked about some of this in the chapter about cleaning your slate and taking out your garbage, but it's such an important part of the process, we are focusing in on your own self-treatment.

Most people have all kinds of hang-ups. Some people also have a low opinion of themselves. People will actually say they are disgusted in themselves, disappointed, have little respect for themselves, and do not particularly like themselves. Some actually live with self-hate.

Living with love toward yourself means having self-respect, self-caring, and loving yourself enough to treat yourself kindly without any self-abuse. Self-abuse is when you call yourself names and hate on yourself for certain mistakes or things you have done. People are very rough on themselves and can be very abusive toward themselves as well.

Living with love toward yourself means changing your perception and treatment of yourself. So, I ask again, "Do you like yourself"? If yes and all you have is love for yourself, then you can skip ahead to the next section. However, if you have any self-guilt, disappointment, or dislike in any way, let's examine that now.

Hopefully you are becoming familiar with my process. If so, you know that you need to very closely look at exactly why you don't feel totally positive or loving toward yourself. Ask yourself what bugs you about yourself. Ask why you feel disappointment in yourself. Ask why

49

you do not love yourself. This is another stare in the mirror moment. Look into your soul. Ask the harsh question. Be honest with yourself even if it is hurtful. Some kind of answer should emerge.

Look the answer squarely in the eyes and face that truth head-on. Feel it, touch it. Then isolate it and break it down into pieces. Is there something specific you did in the past that caused this less than loving opinion of yourself? If so, revert back to the section of this book about wiping the slate clean. Is there something about how you are currently behaving that is causing you to have a less than loving feeling for yourself? If so, then re-visit your Sense of Self design. Is there something else you need to throw in the garbage? Or something else you need modify and adjust? Remember, you are a new person building a new life now. The foundation is clean and solid, and the framing is all up, but you can still make changes to the interior design. So, if there is something bugging you, then fix it.

The process we are in now is basically doing a self-check as to how you feel about yourself. If the answer comes back negative, it means we have to open things up and find the problem. Once we find it, we have to clean it out. Then check yourself again. Do you love yourself? You have to keep going back inside yourself, cleaning and working until your answer is "Yes, I love myself," or at the very least, "Yes, yes, okay, okay, I'm not so horrible, I promise to make friends with myself". I am not expecting perfection, but you can't go forward if you cannot treat yourself with respect and kindness. EVERYONE deserves to be treated with kindness and respect. So that means YOU deserve to be treated that way. If you talk about treating others with love, but treat yourself like crap, then you are a hypocrite. We can't have that. We keep it real here, and we own all our stuff, right?

Once you get to the point where you are willing to be friendly to yourself at the very least, and hopefully loving to yourself, we need to make this your new habitual self-treatment. Be loving and kind to yourself. Give yourself credit for positive things you do. Give yourself rewards for accomplishing tasks. Treat yourself with the same respect you would treat others who deserve respect.

It is very important to treat yourself with love, kindness, and respect, because how we feel inside about ourselves is how we end up treating others. Think about it. People who hate themselves and are always angry, usually treat those around them with anger and are mean. Those who live with self-guilt often project that guilt onto others. Those who are insecure with themselves often project that insecurity onto others and try to make others feel insecure. Those who feel bad about themselves, often try to drag others down to their level as a way of trying to feel better about themselves since misery loves company.

So conversely, those who love and respect themselves will treat others with love and respect. THIS is why living with love toward yourself is so important; and how we treat others leads to our next step in this topic.

LIVING WITH LOVE TOWARD OTHERS

Living with love toward others does not mean you have to love, or even like, everyone. How you FEEL about someone is a result of what kind of a person they are and how they treat you. But how you TREAT someone is totally separate from that and is based upon your method of dealing with people.

A fact of life is that you will get better results from people if you treat them from a place of love. You catch more flies with honey than with vinegar. The whole point of this discussion is to empower you and increase your potential for success and happiness. Part of doing that is for you to learn how to get better results from people you have to live and work with. So yes, this is a positive "love and light" way to live and treat humans, BUT it is also a practical strategy lesson on how to attain better results for yourself in whatever you are trying to accomplish.

Let us all agree that I don't need to write pages and pages about showing love toward those you actually love. Obviously, you don't need help from me loving people you already love. I am not interested in page fillers. I assume you will have no trouble living with love toward people you actually love and like. So how about we just skip ahead to dealing with people we DON'T like very much.

LIVING WITH LOVING OTHERS YOU DON'T LIKE

How do you live with love toward people you do not like? The best way for me to show you this is by giving some practical examples.

Let us say you are dealing with a family member who is not terribly respectful of you. Maybe they are always trying to make you feel bad, point out your flaws, or make sure they pull you below themselves so that they can feel superior. Good one, yes? Most of us have been there. Anyways, most people would end up getting into a fight with this person. You might give them some of their own medicine. You might try to make them feel bad, or make them feel flawed, or make them feel lower than you. You would naturally try to fight back and defend yourself. You are not going to take their crap. You will try to beat them at their own game. All of this will undoubtedly end in a fight, nasty exchange, screaming, and what have you. What will you have accomplished? Anything at all? Nope. Nothing.

Now let's try the same situation by living with love toward others. The family member makes a slight insult at you to gently and not so gently push your buttons. What you say in return is, "OMG you are so funny. I love you because I can always rely on you to say something like that haha. [change subject] By the way, how is your dog Pooky?" Notice in this example I let the insult bounce off me, and I used love to totally disrupt and confuse their insulting flow. Then I totally deflected and diverted. Using this tactic throws the person off their game. They were unable to push your button and you are clearly going to be no fun for them today. On top of that, you used the word "love" toward them, which they had not heard yet that day from anyone. Then you deflected and diverted, by showing interest in what matters to them most (Pooky their dog). The conversation ends with them lost, confused, deflated, and wondering why you are being so nice. Perfect.

Let's try another one. Your A-hole boss calls you into his office. He says you did not do something the way he asked you to do it, even though he never specified how to do it. Normally, you would react by defending yourself and pointing out to him that he never specified how to do it. Furthermore, you point out that you have done it that same way for him before and it was fine. Furthermore, you point out that his assistant told you to do it the way you did it. Well, you showed him, didn't you? Except for the fact that now he hates you even more, and he still wants the item changed. So you leave his office thinking you successfully defended yourself. Instead what you did is make him hate you more, plus now his assistant hates you for dragging them into it, plus you STILL have to do the task all over again to how he wants it.

Now let's try that situation by living with love toward your boss. He says how you screwed up. You look at him. You say in your most calm loving way, "OMG I am so sorry. I feel really bad because I tried so hard to make it how I thought you wanted it. I will fix it for you. You were not around when I started the project, so I was unable to ask you directly. I love when you tell me directly how to do it because you always give clear intelligent instructions, and I totally appreciate that style from you". Then you walk out. So what has happened now? You have caught him by surprise and totally disarmed him. He feels you flattered him, and his ego is feeling fluffy. He loves how pleasant you are when it seemed to him like an annoying day. Not only that, but you may have fixed the problem of getting inaccurate instructions from his assistant by pointing out you prefer getting your instructions directly from the boss. The boss also likes you more now. You will likely get a promotion. You win.

This is too much fun, so let's do one more. Your smart-aleck son who does nothing but talk back to you, has once again not taken out the garbage. Apparently, he ignored Chapter 2 of this book and just refused to take out the garbage as he is supposed to. Normally, you yell his name and he ignores you, so you go to his room and yell at him to take the trash out, and that you are tired of asking him five times, and by the way why is he so irresponsible, etc. He will naturally make some excuse or say something annoying. You will undoubtedly feel your authority is being challenged and you will raise your voice and raise the stakes. It will end with him dragging the leaking trash out, leaving an even bigger mess, and him slamming all doors in the process. Exhausting, yes?

Now let's try the situation living with love. In this case, we obviously do not dislike your son. We love your son. BUT wow, he can be so annoying, exhausting, and irritating. So here is what we try. Instead of yelling his name from the kitchen, you save your breath and walk up to his room. You calmly in a normal voice say, "Hey, you forgot to take the trash out. I would really appreciate it if you could take it now. But when you are done, I want to talk and get caught up on your life this week. I was thinking about you at work today and wondered about so-and-so and such-and-such. Okay. So trash please then let's visit." What will happen here is you have avoided a confrontation by not taking out your knives and swords from the start. You have also disarmed your son by being nice and acting normal. You have also intrigued him by saying you want to chat, get caught up, and visit. He is likely a bit confused and is trying to figure out what is going on. He will be intrigued enough to take the trash out so that he can then talk to you, and figure out what you are up to with wanting to talk to him. You two might even enjoy the talk that follows the trash. Yeah, yeah, kids can be tricky, and you might have to weave, swerve, and modify some of this scenario, but you get the general idea of how to do it.

Living with love toward others is an art. It is almost like a martial art, because you can go into combat with this skill and easily disarm and put your opponent on the floor before they know what happened. Practice it. Consider it a game and hobby to engage in. The bottom line is that coming from a place of love is always better and smarter.

I want you to show love toward yourself because you deserve love.

You deserve to be loved. Everyone deserves to be loved. I want you to show love toward yourself so that you will show love to others. Everyone deserves to be loved. I want you to show love to others so that they will feel loved, and in return show love back to you. Everyone deserves to be loved, and you deserve to be loved. I am writing this book for you so that you can love and be loved.

Chapter Six

Mastering Your Emotions

Being human means having emotions. If you read my book *The Hunter Equation,* you know that having human emotions is one of the greatest and worst things about being human. Emotions are a double-edged sword for sure. In this chapter, we are going to discuss the difference between Experiencing emotions, Controlling emotions, and Expressing emotions.

It is important you are able to clearly understand the differences between the three "modes" I mentioned above. You need to know when to use each, how to use each, and when not to use any of them. I am not trying to make you less human or turn you into a machine. But a highly tuned, effective, and successful person is able to navigate all this to their best advantage. So let's get started.

EXPERIENCING EMOTIONS

Experiencing emotions is a GREAT thing. Anyone who tells you that successful people are stone-cold and have no emotions, is probably a stone-cold person. Having no emotions is not human. Having no emotions means you are a machine. While it is true machines can be very efficient, machines also do not get to experience LIFE.

Experiencing emotions allow us to live a full human experience. We need to experience all the diverse emotions, highs, and lows, that humanity has to offer. It makes us a full well-rounded person. Experiencing a full range of emotions give us depth as a person. Fully experiencing our emotions gives us something infinitely valuable.

Experiencing emotions is what gives us Empathy. Empathy is the most important ingredient for the survival of humanity. Empathy keeps us tuned into our fellow humans so that we don't do undue harm to each other. Without Empathy, we have discrimination, bigotry, war, and genocide. People who don't feel emotion and have no empathy are capable of unspeakable harm.

So we WANT everyone to experience emotions. Unfortunately, many have shut off their emotions. Some at the highest level of power have no emotion because ambition has taken over their entire "sense of self." Some have chosen to have no emotion because they think it has made them more successful in business since they are able to disregard morality without emotion and empathy. Then there are some who are stuck in substance abuse because they no longer wanted to experience emotions, since emotions became too painful.

As you can see, there are plenty of reasons NOT to experience emotions. But the risk and cost of having no emotion is too high. In all the examples above, most of those folks meet an unfortunate ending in some way eventually. And how many people did they hurt along the way, right? But I digress.

My point is that not experiencing emotion is harmful. More importantly, when we don't experience emotion we are missing out on life. Those fleeting moments of amazing emotions makes life worth living. We all know of all our frustrations and suffering, but can also recall a few fleeting moments of feeling on top of the world, or extreme pleasure, satisfaction, and well-being (and I am not talking about what happens in the bedroom).

Hopefully I am making a good case for experiencing emotions. Experience them to the fullest. Fully indulge in life. Fully feel and experience the zest of life. Reach for the emotional experience rather than shutting it off. Experience emotion. But...

CONTROLLING YOUR EMOTIONS

Although I have just spent a lot of effort encouraging you to experience your emotions, it is also essential that you learn to CONTROL your emotions. Think of emotions as nuclear energy inside a nuclear reactor. Very powerful, amazing, and can have huge benefits providing the power of life. But that nuclear reactor must be kept cool and under total control or there will be a meltdown. If your emotions are allowed to run unchecked, you can have a meltdown.

Uncontrolled emotions can cause us huge problems. Negative emotions that constantly remain, or grow in intensity, can lead to depression, substance abuse, or worse. Uncontrolled emotions can cause us to make very bad choices that we regret almost immediately. Uncontrolled emotions can cause us to say things to others that are very hurtful, harmful, and destroy relationships. Basically, uncontrolled emotions that run a-muck can be as harmful as not having any emotions at all. A person with no emotion is a sociopath, but a person with too much uncontrolled emotion can be a lunatic. As with everything in life, there must be BALANCE. You need to enjoy the full experience of emotions, but learn control so that there is no meltdown of your nuclear reactor.

So how do we control emotions? Is there a switch or chip we can buy and install? I wish. There is only one way I know that can be effective in controlling emotions. COPING MECHANISMS. You must develop coping mechanisms for each emotion that work for you. A coping mechanism is something you think of or do in response to an emotion that you wish to control. We will have to go through some examples.

Let's say you want to be able to control the emotion of sadness. Sadness is necessary to experience, but if we experience it too often for too long, it can paralyze us and stop us in our tracks from being productive. We can't have that. Thus, we need to develop a coping mechanism for sadness.

Pretend you have suffered a loss of some sort. You have been sad, you have been grieving, you have been experiencing a healthy amount of emotion for a normal human event. But on this day, you have an important meeting at work. You cannot cancel it and you cannot be a mess and fail at the meeting. The only answer is to control your emotions and get through the meeting. If it were me, I would try a couple of things. Firstly, I would temporarily set aside this current loss. That in itself takes practice to learn to do. But you must set it aside temporarily. Focus on your moment-to-moment tasks, even if it's just brushing your teeth. Just focus on brushing your teeth. Do not let your mind wander. Secondly, think of something fun that you have been looking forward to doing. Start to think of doing that which you have been very excited about doing for a long time. It might be going someplace, getting something, or seeing someone. Focus on your plans for that fun event. Fully immerse your thoughts in it. Then think of your business meeting and what you need to accomplish in that meeting. Fully focus on that meeting and run it through your head step by step, making sure you have all thoughts and preparations in place. Then proceed with your day. If glimpses of sadness come, you must repeat this process or push out those thoughts to the side again. You need to be insistent with yourself, and highly focused.

What I have done above is a form of self-brainwashing and distraction. You are using these coping mechanisms on yourself to control your emotion of sadness. Coping mechanisms are highly personal, so what works for me might not work for you. I am just trying to show you the process and flavor of what you need to come up with. I will give you another example, since we are all sitting here with nothing else to do anyway, right?

Let's say you are feeling very angry. You have been wronged and you are enraged. Unfortunately, you can't stay home and fume, scream, rant, and rave like you want to do and need to do. Instead, you have to rush off to an important meeting. But you are just hating life and everyone in it right now. You just hate everything. You are really upset. How are you going to be effective in your meeting when you are hating everyone and everybody right now?

You will have to use a coping mechanism to control your emotion of anger. The first thing I would do is take some deep breaths. Just like how we had to "set aside" your grieving above, you need to breath out some of this anger and release it out. Lots of deep breaths. Keep doing it until you are actually getting tired. You might even start laughing at yourself because the breathing exercise is so ridiculous. So you have now set aside the anger temporarily through this ridiculous exercise. Now divert your attention. Think of your most loved family member. I don't mean your spouse or partner who was annoying you this morning. What I mean is that little nephew or niece, or that grandchild, or even your own child. Think of that little favorite person that could set the world on fire and you would still love them to death. Yes, that one. Some people might even be able to use a pet for this. But think of them. It's hard to think of them without your mood lightening a bit. You usually smile when you think of this favorite person. So think of them. You can't be angry with them, right? Stay focused on them until you feel you can switch your focus to the business meeting. Then focus on your meeting and go through step by step what you need to do for a successful meeting. Bingo, you have done it again.

In summary, the process of using coping mechanisms is about first setting the trigger or catalyst of the emotion aside. Then you use a diversion tactic. Then you remain in this brainwashed state for as long as needed to control the specified emotion. All of this will take some thought and practice, but it is important and necessary. A person needs to learn to control emotions if they are going to be highly effective and successful. With all that said, we have one more thing to discuss.

EXPRESSING YOUR EMOTIONS

When I talk about "expressing your emotions," I am not talking about when you express the glands of your dog. Although some might say expressing their emotions can be similar. Okay gross. Wow, where do these thoughts come from. Anyway, what I mean by expressing your emotions is how you COMMUNICATE your emotions.

We talked about EXPERIENCING your emotions. Experiencing your emotions is you fully feeling them within yourself. Then we talked about CONTROLLING your emotions. Controlling your emotions is keeping them in check within yourself so that you can function effectively. So far, we have really only talked about what is going on inside you. Now we need to talk about emotions in terms of what happens OUTSIDE yourself. We are talking about how you express or communicate these emotions to others.

In expressing your emotions, you are going to use a combination of experiencing them, along with controlling them. Then add to that, effective communication skills, which take into account Living With Love. Hopefully you can see now what I have been building up to. We did some simple "wax on, wax off" to teach you the basics, but now we are moving into some tricky martial arts combo moves here. As usual, the best way to look at this might be through running some scenarios.

Let's say you are very angry at your sibling for something they said. You love your sibling and deep down you know it was a mistake, but what they said was very hurtful and even harmful to you. You are very angry. You are going to experience that anger because it's normal and natural. You need to be allowed to fully feel and experience this anger because it would be unhealthy to repress it. But you cannot let it eat you alive inside. So you use some coping mechanisms to keep yourself calm. You can't be boiling over and acting like a crazy lunatic or be seen as overly dramatic. So you use the release/set aside trick, along with the diversion method, to remain in control of the anger. But now you need to talk to your sibling about what they did to you. You need to express your emotions. You need to communicate your emotions to them. But you need to do this while living in love.

You might say to your sibling, "I really need to talk to you about something that is really hurting me. I have been very upset and angry about what you said. I could barely sleep and eat I was so angry. I hate being this angry and I hate being angry with YOU. What hurt me the most is what you said is not true because so-on and so-forth. I really want to also hear how you feel about this, now that I have expressed my feelings to you." Then you wait for their response and go back-and-forth as needed.

You will see above I used all the elements. You fully felt the emotion of anger as a healthy normal person would. But you used your coping mechanisms to control it in a reasonable way. You then expressed your emotion in an accurate effective way, while doing it in a loving way. Your sibling's reaction should be one of respecting your feelings and listening, because you did not just all out attack them like a lunatic. You were so calm and sounded well thought out, that they are likely a bit scared of what they did because you are taking it so seriously. Thus, they will now take it seriously also. Plus, you made them feel bad because you are being kind, respectful, and even loving to them, while they did not show you the same consideration. So it is safe to say at this point you have taken the high road and should expect some fairly good results. Certainly, your results will be better than if you had just lost control and acted all crazy, and made all parties more upset than they already were.

This is a very highly person thing. I will not bore you with endless examples that don't apply to you exactly. Your situations will be very different I'm sure. But it is important you develop this process of expressing your emotions.

I will be the first to admit that entire books can be written about Mastering Your Emotions. Definitely, I have not covered everything. But I feel confident I have given you plenty to chew on. Please consider all I have said and re-read this chapter when needed. Mastering your emotions is easier said than done, but is the true mark of a Jedi.

Chapter Seven
Morality

What is Morality? Wikipedia defines Morality this way: Morality (from Latin: *moralis*, lit. 'manner, character, proper behavior') is the differentiation of intentions, decisions and actions between those that are distinguished as proper and those that are improper. Morality can be a body of standards or principles derived from a code of conduct from a particular philosophy, religion, or culture, or it can derive from a standard that a person believes should be universal.

If you permit me, I am going to reduce this equation-like definition to: Morality is a body of standards or principles derived from a code of conduct society or a person deems as proper or correct behavior.

Or, if you permit me further, I will say Morality is knowing right from wrong. For our purposes, we will use the positive nature of it and say **Morality is knowing and doing what is right.** Phew. Glad we cleared that up.

A well-functioning society has to have morality, otherwise we would have chaos and injustice. However, as you know, there are many people in our society who are not moral. There are people that simply do not care about doing what is right. Such people will do anything they want regardless of moral standing or who their actions hurt. Such people do not belong in a highly evolved civilized society. Such people are also what I call "empty souls."

I believe people with no morality are broken. They have had some sort of damage and trauma that broke them and caused them to lose their morality. My experience is that such people end up suffering and living real consequences from their lack of morality. We do not want to end up like them.

THE LIFE CYCLE OF MORALITY

I believe Morality actually has a life cycle to it. By examining this, we can try to understand it better before we apply it directly to ourselves.

I believe all humans are born with Empathy. Yes, there are exceptions, genetic mutations, and so on, but for this discussion I am going to stick to the huge majority rather than getting lost in the weeds with exceptions. Thus, for the sake of this argument, I believe Empathy is within all humans upon birth. We are also going to define Empathy as the ability to feel, relate to, and identify with another's feelings and circumstances. This is why we say, "sympathize" when we feel sorry for someone, but we say, "empathize" when we can actually FEEL for them and understand on an emotional level.

So if all humans are born with empathy, then what in the world goes wrong? I believe things start to go wrong quite quickly. A human born with empathy will naturally expect others to treat them the way they would like to be treated, since the definition of empathy is for one person to understand and feel what the other is feeling. I think what happens is that early on, the child has some negative experiences where they realize others do not always truly understand them, feel them, or are able to anticipate their needs or feelings. These probably innocent negative experiences begin to foster a confusion and distrust in the child's understanding of empathy. The child begins to question if the empathy they were born with is actually real and reciprocal, or just a false illusion.

These doubts are soon dipped in concrete when they experience situations where others purposely do things to hurt them. This can happen at any point in the process during their young life. For example, it could be when a parent or family member abuses them in some way. Or it might happen in school when other children intentionally do things to hurt them. The child soon fully realizes that empathy is not a universal law and is in fact a vulnerability.

Depending on how many negative events a child experiences, or the severity of the events, a child can begin to naturally lose their empathy. They realize people do not have empathy for them, so why should they have empathy for others. They even feel empathy is a weakness and a chink in their armor. Phrases like "Don't wear your heart on your sleeve" don't help either.

By the time a person has entered young adulthood, they have learned empathy is not guaranteed and possibly even rare. They have learned to live not expecting empathy. They likely have also stopped giving empathy to others. However, during the teen years, something magic usually happens. A person meets someone special. They fall in love. The person they fall in love with shows them empathy in its highest form. This high dose of empathy is amazing, addicting, and wonderful, and makes a person think that this horrible world can actually be an amazing place if with the right person who gives a level of caring and empathy they have not experienced before.

At this point, the young adult has seen both sides of the coin. They have been born with empathy, but also had it quickly stripped away. They have become used to a world with little empathy. But now they have also seen a world with amazing large amounts of empathy from their first love. But of course, first loves usually crumble eventually, and the large amount of empathy goes with it. The young person realizes empathy is fickle and comes and goes, and is wonderful, but also a weakness.

Enter stage right the young person's introduction to the working world. They learn very quickly there is almost no empathy in the dog-eat-dog world of business and career. In fact, depending on what industry they are in, they learn that empathy is actually a total weakness and to be avoided at all costs. The world of "greed is good," "sell them at any cost," "tell them what they want to hear," and so on is there new reality. At this point, a very ambitious young person can decide to completely discard any notion or remnants of empathy they may have had, because they have decided that it is completely useless and irrelevant in their world. And that's that.

After this point, everyone's journey is very different. Some people remain without empathy their entire life. Others meet new special people, find empathy again, and embrace it. Others have awakenings and realize that having empathy gives them peace and happiness in their lives. People sometimes find their way, and sometimes people never find their way. And here we sit. Some people have huge amounts of empathy, and others have none.

I believe empathy exists within people on a sliding scale. Imagine a scale from 0 to 10. A "0" on the empathy scale would be someone with no empathy at all. This would be an extreme sociopath who is dangerous to humanity. Hitler is a great example of this. They will kill for no reason with absolutely no regard and no thought for their victim. Feelings do not even register within the person's mind because they have zero empathy.

Conversely, someone with an empathy score of "10" on our scale would be someone who has large amounts of empathy for everyone and everything. This person will wreck their car in order to avoid hitting a squirrel. This person actually feels pain when a tree gets cut down. This person feels the pain of everyone and everything around them. They are amazingly nice and generous people. BUT, they tend to be overly generous to their own detriment. They are easily taken advantage of, and are constant victims of people using them, and indeed taking advantage of them.

So while the person with an empathy score of 0 is a monster, the person with an empathy score of 10 is highly vulnerable, and usually struggles through life on many levels. Thus, the sweet spot is to be somewhere in the middle of the empathy scale. But what part of the middle?

For example, a person with an empathy score of 4 is likely that mean boss who is "fair," but won't go out of his way for anyone. Someone with a score of 8 is a very nice person who might seem a bit naive as they fall for scams now and again. So where should a person be? 5? 6? 7? That is up to you. FINALLY, we are getting to the point of this chapter. YOU have to decide where on the scale you want to be. As long as you are somewhere in the middle, there are no wrong answers.

I mentioned in an earlier chapter that a successful used car salesperson might need to be a bit lower on the morality scale to accommodate for some exaggerations and omissions of facts in order to survive their job. Like-wise, a person in charge of admissions for a University will have to keep their empathy lower so they can evaluate candidates based on qualifications, rather than their personal feelings for them. However, someone who is a counselor had best be very high on the empathy scale or they will not be able to do their job well. So where you are on the scale will depend somewhat on what you do and whom you spend your time with.

For example, if you are surrounded by narcissists and business sharks, you might want to remain a bit lower on the scale because you have to watch your back and be somewhat cynical to survive. Conversely, if you are surrounded by a loving tribe of friends and like-minded individuals, you will need to remain higher on the scale to match the higher vibration around you.

Myself, I find I am able to adjust my empathy level according to the environment I find myself in. I can truly turn it all the way up so that I am feeling the grass, but I can also turn it way down if I am dealing with someone who I know is trying to do me harm and take advantage of me. This is why genuinely good people might have a good opinion of me, but jerks often will tell you I am horrible. It is because I can match my empathy and behavior to the environment in which I find myself, or the person with whom I find myself.

THE IMPORTANCE OF MORALITY

As you can see, I have equated Morality with Empathy. Empathy is the basis for having a conscience, and a conscience is what leads to a sense or standard of morality. I also spent a good amount of time explaining how a person's empathy, and thus morality, can slide up and down on a scale. So why does it matter to have morality?

Many of us have learned the secret already. We have realized that having a higher sense of morality leads to a higher level of happiness and inner peace within ourselves. Is this because being a good person makes us feel better? Yes. But I believe it is more than that. I believe having a high level of morality means we have a high level of empathy, which brings us back to our original roots as an innocent human. Having a strong sense of morality gives us a strong feeling of humanity. It is this strong sense of humanity, or positive humanity, which fills in our circle and gives us a sense of peace and well-being.

That is why in the process of Rising To Greatness, I believe it is helpful to have a very strong sense of morality and high moral standards. I believe it adds to your fulfillment and happiness in the long run. It's just natural we want to be a good person. When we KNOW we are a good person, it is a self-validation that completes us. That contributes to our happiness and success as a person.

So what level of morality/empathy should you ultimately have? That is up to you to answer. All I will tell you from my own personal experience is that I've met some really decent smart people at around a 6, and I've also met amazing people who can function effectively at a 9. Where you want to be is up to you and what works best for you. The point of this chapter was to give clarity to this very important subject, so that you can be fully aware of your own morality. A person

69

can also always change if they decide they want to. One thing for sure is that we need more morality in this world. I suggest you be what you would like to see in the world.

Chapter Eight
Motivation

Without motivation not much gets done. Humans naturally need some sort of incentive, need, or compulsion to do things. Usually there is a desire or a need, and then that spawns Motivation. Thus, there are two sides to motivation. There is the negative side that usually stems from a NEED. The motivation is that if we don't do something or get something, then something bad will happen to us. For example, we are highly motivated to earn money for food so that we don't starve to death. We are motivated so that we can avoid bad things happening to us. This type of motivation is no fun at all.

Then there is positive motivation, which usually stems from an incentive. The motivation is that IF you do something, you GET something in return. For example, we might be highly motivated to earn money so we can buy that new car we want. This motivation results from a very strong incentive. This motivation is obviously more fun and encouraging. In this chapter, I am going to focus on this more positive incentive-based type of motivation.

Why is motivation important in your process of Rising To Greatness? The whole point of your transformation is to BECOME greater than you are. You are trying to achieve something. We know if we become greater, we can live a more meaningful, happy life full of more success and the things we have always wanted in our lives. In order to get through this transformation and achieve all of our goals, we have a lot of work to do. A critical element in surviving all of the work we are doing, and the work yet to come, is to have large amounts of motivation to keep us going. If we lack in motivation, we will lose the incentive, compulsion, and energy to continue the fight. The dream could die. For this reason, Motivation is a required ingredient for any person who becomes great or achieves greatness.

Here is the bottom line. The greater, bigger, more powerful, your sense of motivation, the greater your chances of success and reaching your goals. It's really that simple. So, the no-brainer is to build the biggest most efficient motivation machine you can possibly create. So, let's do that.

GOAL SETTING

All my experiences have shown me that the most important elements for successful motivation are the following elements of goal setting:
1. An extremely clear goal
2. A very well-lit clear pathway to the goal
3. A clearly defined structure of goal posts that must be reached along the way (I call them "dots")
4. The "dots" must not be spread too far apart
5. The process of connecting the dots to create a clear pathway must be constructed starting with the end result goal and working backwards to your present starting point (reverse engineering).

72

I believe the best way for us to proceed is for me to walk you through the entire process from start to finish. Before we begin, let me remind you and make it clear that the key to MOTIVATION is having a positive incentive (goal) to reach for. Motivation is what DRIVES US to keep going until we reach that desired result.

Therefore, the first step in the process is to create a very clear, specific, strong incentive. This is your GOAL. This is your desired result. What do you want? What do you want to achieve? What do you want to do? You must answer this. Search your heart, your mind, your soul, and your deepest desires. What is your inspiration? What drives your existence? What would truly better your life? Come up with your goal, your desired result. You must clearly define it and envision it. Without being clearly defined or envisioned in your mind's eye, you will not succeed. You must fully understand and see your desired result in 3D HD full color and surround-sound.

Many people find it helpful to construct a "vision board." A vision board is an actual board or paper, where you write down, or even paste pictures, of your desired result. It helps to make your goals more real and concrete. Write your envisioned goal and desired result on paper, or make a poster board of it, complete with cut out pictures. This process can also make you realize that you are forgetting or leaving out certain details, which you can add to make the goal complete.

Then, in your mind, sit at your goal. Sit at your end-result in your mind. Bathe in it. Be in it as if it was present day. Feel it, touch it, smell it, live it. It should feel real to you. You should see all its details and features. Spend some time at your desired destination. This allows you to become more familiar with what you will be fighting for. It confirms that you actually want this desired result. It should also get you more excited to work for it and achieve it. Now for the next step in the process.

While you are sitting at your desired end-result, draw a line in your mind from that end-point back to where you actually are in present day. Now you have a pathway from your desired result back to where you stand in present day. This will be your general compass guide to get from point B back to point A. I am basically using reverse engineering.

Now what you need to do next is set up mini goal posts (dots) at regular intervals from point B to point A. So, what you are doing is working backwards from the end-goal back to where you stand in present day. These "mini goal posts" (or dots) are in actuality the concrete steps, actions, and achievements you must complete in order to reach your goal.

I personally prefer to start at the end-goal and work backwards, using this reverse engineering. But if this is too confusing for you and you would prefer to start where you are now and work forward, that is fine. Just remember to use that imaginary line from Point B to Point A as your general guideline of where to set up your mini goal posts.

Create your list of mini goal posts. Ask yourself, "What steps must I take in order to reach my goal"? This question will force you to write down a list of steps you must take and achieve in order to reach your goal. Each of these steps you write down is a mini goal post, or dot. Work carefully to come up with a realistic, accurate, and doable list of steps to achieve your goal. This is like baking a cake. You must first procure all required ingredients. Procuring each ingredient is in itself a step in the process. Then after you have all the ingredients, you must follow step-by-step instructions (in correct order) to make the cake. Follow the same process for creating your list of steps for reaching your goal. Now you have a list of steps (mini goal posts or dots) which are required for reaching your goal.

Starting at either Point B OR Point A (whichever you preferred), start laying out your mini goals posts along the line that connects point A and point B. Obviously, the goal posts must be put in the correct order on the line. When you are finished, you should have all your steps (mini goal posts) laid out in order on the line so that STEP 1 is located very close to your present starting location. The last step in reaching your goal will be located very close to point B, which is your end-goal desired result.

This is a VERY IMPORTANT point. Your mini goal posts (dots)

must not be spread too far apart. In other words, make sure each step in reaching your goal is more of a baby step. You want very little distance between your steps (mini goal posts). This is probably the most critical part in maintaining strong motivation. If the steps are spread too far apart, you risk getting discouraged and losing motivation.

USING MOTIVATION TO CONNECT THE DOTS

I don't know about you, but that last section has left me feeling like I am building some big complicated piece of furniture from IKEA or those assemble the furniture yourself places. Phew. But we did it. You have a clear well-defined pathway to your clear well-defined goal, with clear well-defined steps located close together between your present location and your end-goal.

All that is left to do now is walk the pathway. Walk to each step. You are now walking to each "dot," and then connecting the dots by walking from dot to dot. This is no longer imaginary. This is real. This is you actually completing actions to reach each step. It's hard work. It is not easy. But you can make it.

You can make it because you are motivated by a great incentive. You have that desired result at the end of the road to look forward to. You have a clear path to follow so you won't get lost in the woods. If you can just remain on that path and reach each mini goal post (dot), you are guaranteed to reach your end-goal. The mental motivational trick at this point is to only think of two things. The first thing you never want to forget is that much desired end-goal. Always keep it in mind. The second thing you want to focus on is THE NEXT STEP, the next mini goal post. Convince yourself and realize that reaching that next step IS your key to success. A house is not built all at once. A house is built one wall at a time, one block at a time. Don't focus on that long climb up the hill with ALL THOSE steps and mini goal posts. FORGET all of those mini goal posts and steps. Only think of two things: The Promised Land at the top, and the nearest next step or goal post you must reach. Stare at that next mini goal post. We spaced them very close together so that you can see each one very clearly from where you stand. It's not that far. You can see it. Walk to it. Don't give up. Don't look to the side. Don't look back. Don't look at all the other steps ahead. Just look at the next one you are walking to.

This is the thinking and mentality you will use during the entire journey. You have essentially broken the journey down into many tiny steps. You just have to focus on the next tiny step ahead of you, while still thinking of that wonderful end-result at the very end.

MOTIVATION WHEN THINGS GET ROUGH

Nobody promised this would be easy. There are times we get discouraged, tired, or have setbacks. If you find yourself tired, with sore feet, lying on the side of the path hoping someone runs you over, here are some tricks.

Sometimes it is helpful to take a break. Do something else. Disconnect from your journey in your mind. Go for a walk or take a day trip. We all need breaks. Sometimes all we need is a little time off to reset.

What works for me is to re-connect very deeply to my end-goal desired result. Remember when I had you "bathe" in your end goal? I had you fully immerse yourself in it so you could feel it, touch it, smell it, and fully experience it. Put yourself back in that place. Re-connect to it. Spend some time at Point B. Pack a lunch and hang out there a while. Yes, it's a fantasy, but it reminds you of what you are fighting for and it can re-invigorate you. It reminds you how badly you want that end-goal and why it's worth the pain and effort. I also use music during this process, as it seems to intensify my experience in connecting to my end-goal.

Another trick is to create some sub-steps between your original steps, or dots. Sometimes when we are tired, those baby steps we set up are too far apart. So if needed, break the pathway down into even smaller steps. You might only need to do this temporarily or in a certain section of the pathway until you get your momentum back again.

What I also like to do is use tiny rewards to reach points between the steps. This would be similar to treating yourself to a snack or beverage at certain intervals between your steps. Be kind to yourself. Encourage yourself. Throw yourself a bone. This is called MOTIVATION. You are motivating yourself.

The ability to motivate yourself is one of the most important tools you will keep in your toolbox we are building. You must fully understand motivation and be able to motivate yourself to achieve your desired results.

MOTIVATING OTHERS

Equally important, is knowing how to motivate others. This ability is not just for professional managers. This skill is needed by everyone. The reason is that there will always be goals and tasks you need to complete that involve other people. Your life will be much easier if you are competent at motivating others to your advantage.

I am obviously not going to torture you by repeating the goal setting and motivational process all over again for the subject of motivating others. So let me just point out the key points that are different, or must be added, when motivating others.

The most important factor in motivating others is to realize that your end-goal might not be THEIR end-goal. So you must identify an end-goal and incentive that motivates the other person. Different people respond to different things. Some people are all about money and that's it. Other people respond better to personal recognition and respect. You need to determine what excites the person most and structure your incentive for them accordingly. The incentive must be effective for them or you will not be able to motivate them. That is really the biggest trick.

The next trick is that you will need to build their pathway and mini goal posts for them. Unless they have read this book, they might not be as clever as you at building pathways and mini goal posts to reach end-goals effectively. So you need to build all this for them so they have a clear path with clear mini goal posts stacked close together for them to easily reach and achieve.

After you have put an effective end-goal incentive ahead of them and built a good pathway with correct mini goal posts, all that is left is for you to be a cheerleader. You will need to remind them of their incentive and keep them encouraged. If they get tired or discouraged, you might have to throw them an extra incentive between the baby steps to keep them going or re-boot them.

The key to motivating others is to show plenty of empathy in truly understanding what will motivate them and show caring in how you encourage them along the way. Living with love while you motivate others using empathy.

Chapter Nine
Discipline

I f you look up "Discipline" in the dictionary, you are likely to find this definition: "the practice of training people to obey rules or a code of behavior, using punishment to correct disobedience." This is not the definition we will be using for this book. Again, I find myself in the position of having to use the variant definition. I would define "Discipline" as: The ability to stick with a fixed plan or regimen. For our purposes, I do not see Discipline as a training practice involving punishment. That type of discipline is not very effective anyway, but that's a different topic for another time. I see Discipline as a TOOL, ABILITY, and SKILL to be used to stay with a certain plan you have laid out for yourself.

Thus, I view Discipline as another tool we are about to add to your toolbox for success. Every successful person has discipline of some sort. You can have the greatest plans and talents, but if you lack the discipline to fully carry out your plan and apply your talents, you will not make it to the finish line.

Undoubtedly, distractions and discouragements will crop up to derail your fine-tuned plans. Human frailties like feeling tired and annoyed will also distract us from our path. Humans are by nature creatures of comfort. We do not like to wake up, get out of bed, and do difficult work or tasks when we are not in the mood.

Discipline is basically the ability to do everything you are supposed to do, regardless of your human moods, frailties, and outside distractions. Discipline keeps us on track and on task. Discipline is critical to the completion of any task, plan, or journey.

I first need to point out there are two types of discipline for our purposes. There is Discipline of Action and Discipline of Strategy. Discipline of Action is the ability to keep fixed and focused on a specific task. Discipline of Strategy is to keep fixed and focused on a specific plan of actions or idea.

Discipline of Action is the typical definition or type of discipline you likely had in mind. A person has a set task or plan they must carry out, and they engage discipline to makes sure they keep working until they complete the task.

Discipline of Action is all about focusing on the ACTION of completing the task. It is more about shutting out your human frailties and just focusing on your task, and never stopping until you are done.

Discipline of Strategy is very different. This type of Discipline is your ability to stick to a plan, idea, or strategy you had. Rather than action or physical based, Discipline of Strategy is all mental and emotional based. A person has made a solid decision to do something, but then some human fear, doubt, or discouragement creeps in which makes the person stop.

Discipline of Strategy is your ability to push past these mental hurdles and continue on your well thought out mission.

THE BUILDING BLOCKS OF DISCIPLINE

Discipline consists of the following ingredients:

1. Clear correct mission
2. Solid structure of rules, policies, and procedures
3. Fixed schedule
4. Focus

All four of these elements are essential in order for Discipline to be effective. I will break down each and discuss.

CLEAR CORRECT MISSION

A clear correct mission is the foundation for discipline. This is because without a clear correct mission, you will surely lose your way, lose faith, have doubts, and simply give up. So what is a "clear correct mission" anyway?

A clear correct mission is your task or idea to be completed. It can be painting steps, writing a report, or building a business. Whatever it is, the task must be CLEARLY defined and specific. You have to know exactly what you intend to do and want to do. This obviously relates back to the goal setting we discussed previously. So you must have a clearly thought out task and plan with all the ingredients required and all the steps mapped out. If you do not have clarity of the task at hand, you will have confusion and doubts. Confusion and doubts kill discipline.

Next, you must have a CORRECT mission or task. What I mean by this is that you have truly decided this task needs to be completed, or you truly want it completed. You need to have determined that this task is worthy of your time and effort. You need to know that the task is correctly designed and planned. You need to confirm that the task does not violate your morals or values. All of this is important because if the mission or task does not pass any of these tests, you will end up with doubts, questions, confusion, and your discipline will fail.

For example, imagine you start painting your steps. You get halfway through and you are very tired as it's a lot of work and hurting your back. In this moment of tired weakness, you look at the steps and question whether you made the correct color choice. Your mind will start to mess with you at this point. Your mind will start to convince you that maybe you chose the wrong color. Your mind will use this doubt as an excuse of why you should stop painting. Your mind will use this doubt as an excuse to kill your discipline and cause you to not complete the task. Therefore, it is essential that you made sure the color you chose was absolutely the correct color. If you choose your color carefully, then when this doubt regarding the color comes up halfway during the job, your mind will say, "No, I chose this color carefully and this is the color it is going to be," and your discipline will continue to carry you through to the finish line.

Let's do one more example, except this time involve "Discipline of Strategy" regarding an idea. Much more vague and tricky! Pretend you decided to start a business. You came up with a very clear correct mission. You very carefully thought out exactly what the business would do. You very carefully thought out why you are doing the business, and decided it was definitely best for you and your family. As everyone who has started a business knows, some weeks or months can go by and life gets tough. Things are not quick and easy. The doubts start sneaking into your mind. These doubts and fears start to question your decision to start this business. These doubts make you think about giving up. In other words, your discipline to carry through your plan of successfully starting this business start to be at risk. You are now thinking of giving up. This is exactly when you need to rely on the fact that your still clear plan was CORRECT. You need to remind yourself that you spent a lot of time and thought making sure this mission was CORRECT. Remind yourself of all the contemplation, and your calculations regarding how this would benefit your family and yourself in the long run. You must at this point have faith in your assessment that your clear mission IS CORRECT. Knowing your mission is correct allows you to push back the doubts and stop them from killing your discipline in continuing your hard work.

You can see by now that a clear correct mission is the foundation upon which discipline stands. Now we will look at the actual moving parts of discipline.

STRUCTURE OF RULES, POLICIES & PROCEDURES

A solid structure of rules, policies, and procedures is the life-blood of discipline. To me, this is what discipline is all about. This is what makes discipline work. If you only remember one thing about discipline, make sure it is this section.

Once you have your clear correct mission, you need to decide how you want to accomplish it. This will obviously depend on what exactly your task or mission is. But at this point, it becomes a matter of DOING the tasks. So your discipline is simply DOING the tasks without giving up. In order to do this, you come up with your plan on how you will complete the tasks.

Create a list of rules, policies, and procedures. For example, a rule might be "Once I start a certain task within the mission, I won't stop until it's completed," or "I have to get to step 3 before I can have lunch", or "I have to complete 5 steps of the task before I can go to bed". You basically set down the law for yourself. You make rules you must follow. This is discipline. FOLLOW THE RULES. The rules must be realistic, doable, and in concrete.

What I mean by "Policies" is that you come up with contingency rules for your rules. For example, "In the event I break my leg while completing step 1, I will take a 5 minute rest, then will complete the task using my other good leg." Policies are meant to be other rules you follow should certain events arise. Policies are meant to plug any holes or chances of EXCUSES creeping in. When something unexpected or difficult crops up, you should have a Policy on how you will proceed. So policies are rules that are above or below the original more major rules.

"Procedures" are the order in which you institute rules and policies. You will do certain things in a certain order. "If a step breaks while I am painting it, I will stop painting, repair the step, and then resume painting." The Policy on this might be "If a step breaks and I become delayed fixing it, I may reduce my required number of steps to paint before bedtime by three."

The entire point of rules, policies, and procedures is so that you brainlessly follow the rules without any doubts or excuses being able to creep in. You don't have to make judgments during weak moments of being tired or discouraged. Just follow the rules! Very simple. Discipline! The next element we will discuss is another very helpful coping tool used in discipline.

FIXED SCHEDULE

Very much related to having rules, polices, and procedures, is having a fixed schedule. The rules, policies, and procedures are the structure of discipline. Having a Fixed Schedule is the movement within the structure. The Fixed Schedule dictates at what rate you will perform the tasks. A schedule is essential to discipline. Without a schedule, discipline becomes too open-ended and vulnerable to cheating.

For example, if you have the task of painting the steps, you might be ready to follow your rules and complete the mission, but you might cheat the system by delaying your start time, or cutting out workdays all together. Having a fixed schedule means you can't cheat. If your schedule indicates that you start at 8:00AM, then you need to start at 8:00AM. I highly advise you take your schedule very seriously. I do. It's no joke. This is part of discipline. If you cannot show up on time, then you have no discipline and you will fail. To succeed you must have discipline, and to have discipline, you must have a fixed schedule, and that means you must show up on time.

Having a fixed schedule is useful in all parts of your life, especially if you are self-employed. I know plenty of self-employed people who still wake up to an alarm clock **and** start work at a specific time. Doing this is engaging discipline and one reason for their success. If you have problems with motivation or laziness, then sticking to a fixed schedule can be an effective cure for your illness. If you stick to a specific schedule, then it does not matter how lazy you are, because you are forced to do the tasks on the correct time frame.

I find that the more strict I am with my schedule, the more disciplined I am. The more disciplined I am, the productive I am. The more productive I am, the more successful I become.

FOCUS

Finally, we have the last element in discipline. Focus is the glue that keeps everything together. It is also the grease that keeps everything moving. If you have done the hard work of having created a clear correct mission, and have put in strong rules, policies, and procedures, and you are sticking to a fixed schedule, then all you need to do now is FOCUS on all of that. Everything up to the Focus part of it is about building the structure of your discipline. The Focus element is the mental game portion. It is the "brainwashing" portion of discipline. Focus means only thinking about the task at hand. Focus means only following the rules. Focus means making sure you adhere to the schedule. Focus is the brainless task of just following the structure you put into place.

Focus is not only a critical element of discipline, but it is also the best coping mechanism you have available. Focusing allows you to block out all possible doubts, questions, and excuses. Focus is that blocking mechanism to be sure nothing sways you off your path. Focus is about trusting that your structure is sound. Having a strong focus will prevent your discipline from failing because focus does not allow room for failure.

Discipline is an amazing tool. Many people hate discipline and always sigh when they hear the word. I LOVE discipline! I would have to say discipline is one of the reasons for any successes I have had in my life. If you embrace discipline, it will become your greatest tool and best friend.

Chapter Ten
Believing In Yourself

U p to this point, we have been focusing on your basic structure and filling your toolbox with tools. This chapter is a way of taking a time-out and doing a reality check. At his point in the process, you really should have enough basic skills and structure to feel that you can believe in yourself. So, do you believe in yourself?

Oh wait, don't answer that yet. We should first clearly define what we mean by believing in ourselves. For our purposes here, believing in yourself means two things:

1. Having full confidence that you possess the self-awareness and abilities, we have outlined so far in this book.
2. Having full confidence in your abilities to complete a task or goal for which you are qualified to complete.

I am not going to repeat everything we have covered so far in this book, but let me list a few bullet points as a reminder:

- The past is in the past and your new life is now
- You know who you are with your Sense Of Self
- You are capable of setting aside or eliminating fear in order to accomplish anything
- You are capable of living with love, even if you are not feeling the love in certain moments
- You are able to control your emotions, so they do not interfere with your tasks or goals
- You have a definite structure of morals and values
- You are able to motivate yourself sufficiently to accomplish any task or goal you set
- You have the discipline to follow through on any task or plan you decide to accomplish

The above is obviously an EXTREME ABREVIATION of what we have covered. My only point in listing those was to show you that at this point you should have the capacity to know who you are, where you stand, what you can do, and that you can complete your mission once you decide to do it. In other words, you believe in yourself. Now some of you might be saying, "Yeah I believe in myself, get on with it already." Others of you might be saying, "Yeah but wait, I was just reading all this now and still digesting it." Others might be saying, "I read it all but still feel unsure of things." You all need to hang in there. We will get through this fast, but it's important.

So, do you believe in yourself? You need to, and you should. Just by the fact you have engaged with this book and each chapter shows willingness, and the fact you have gotten this far in our process shows you are able. However, we need total clarity on this issue. So for those who are not certain, or anyone with the slightest wobble or doubt, let us drill down on this now.

As is often the case, I prefer to work the problem backwards.

88

Therefore, if you cannot say without hesitation that you totally believe in yourself, let's identify why. When you ask yourself if you believe in yourself and you do not get an immediate "yes," why is that? Is it because of a past trauma, which led to self-esteem issues? Is it because of one skill you feel you are lacking? There is one fairly easy way to identify this. Go backwards in this book and identify which chapter contains the item you doubt. There must be one section, item, or chapter you have read so far that you did not conquer or accept with 100% certainly. Which one is it?

Obviously, it would be easier if I were there with you. You could tell me which chapter contains your remaining doubt, and we could flush it out and resolve it. But I am here, and you are there. So you will need to use everything we have learned so far to identify it, isolate it, and pull it out for examination. Another way to do this is to ask yourself a question. Right now, thinking about this chapter, what would you say are your biggest weaknesses or vulnerabilities? What is your greatest weakness that prevents you from believing in yourself? Write it down. Then take that item and go back to Chapter 2. Glance or skim through Chapter 2 again but keeping the weakness you wrote down in the forefront of your mind. Run your weakness through our process again. These weaknesses are like bugs. You can spray once and most of them die. But very often you have to spray a second time to get the stragglers. So, spray a second time. This is yet another opportunity to take out more garbage. Remember, one of the themes of this book is that everyone deserves a chance. Everyone deserves a second chance. Everyone deserves a third, fourth, fifth chance, or more until you achieve the success you were looking for. We have nothing but patience and love for you. We all want you to succeed. Nobody left behind. Everyone is important and has value. So let's go back and fix this.

List ANY AND ALL reasons why you do not believe in yourself 100%. List them all down. Then go back and remove the debris and garbage. Forgive yourself. Fix what you can, but then move on from the rest. Leave the past and move forward in the present and future now. This is all a process of healing and building. Healing takes time and many tries sometimes. Go back, spray those bugs, and clean out the debris and garbage as many times as it takes. Even if you have to read those chapters 100 times, it's fine. There is only ONE THING that matters here. What matters is that YOU succeed, prevail, and Rise To Greatness. Have love and patience for yourself in this process.

I will tell you something else. Those who wrestle with the alligator in the mud most often become the strongest. So if you struggle and have to revisit certain issues numerous times, it likely means that when you finally conquer the issue, it is more likely to stick. You will have spent more time rooting it out and scraping yourself clean. Thus, your efforts are not in vain.

You must believe in yourself. This is what makes you powerful. This is going to be the firewall of protection for what comes next. We will be discussing the difficulties in communicating with others, negotiating with others, dealing with toxic people, and many complexities that will require you to have no self-doubts. You need to have a solid wall that will not crumble. This is all about truly believing in yourself.

The Universe, life, and people, will throw all kinds of things at you in an effort to confuse you, weaken you, manipulate you, and take advantage of you. Those who are "weak" fall victim. Do you know what the definition of "weak" is? "Weak" means not believing in yourself. Weak does not mean you lack big muscles or a loud voice. Weak means you are unsure of yourself. Weak means you easily crumble because you are susceptible to doubts. Weak means you won't assert yourself because you have doubts. You have doubts because you do not believe in yourself.

Believing in yourself does not mean you know everything, or are always right, or never make mistakes. Believing in yourself does not mean you are perfect without flaws. You will still have lapses in your knowledge base. You will still have things you are not good at. You will still make mistakes. Believing in yourself means that despite all your flaws and mistakes, you STILL know who you are, what you stand for, what you like, what you don't like, where you are going, and how you want to get there. Believing in yourself is knowing yourself. Believing in yourself is knowing you have value and worth. Believing in yourself is knowing you can apply yourself and accomplish goals you put forth.

If you asked me if I believe in you in, I would look at you. I would ask if you know who you are and what you stand for. I would ask if you are not afraid to set goals and complete the tasks required to reach those goals. If you answered those correctly, I would tell you that I believe in you. But it would not be relevant. You do not need my validation. You do not need anyone else's validation. You only need to believe in yourself.

Chapter Eleven
Master Communicator

Onward we go in filling your toolbox with more tools. Communication is one of the most essential tools for navigating everything in life. Whether it is business or personal relationships, you must be able to communicate effectively. There are some slight differences between communicating in the business world and in your personal relationships, and I will attempt to highlight some of those differences.

But first, let me just give you the big secret up front. The secret to being a Master Communicator, is being a Master Listener. If you have not already noticed, I tend to work every problem and every situation backwards with reverse engineering. Communicating is no different.

Instead of thinking what I am going to say, I first listen to the other person and figure them out, THEN I think about what I am going to say. So, to me communicating is not really about talking. Communicating is about listening.

When most people speak or communicate, they are doing it from a selfish perspective. What I mean is that a person has something they feel compelled to express, and they need to say it and express it so they can feel better. Expressing themselves and saying what they want to say makes them feel better. They are communicating or speaking for their own benefit. This creates a problem when you have two people both having compelling urges to express themselves and say things. What happens is the two people end up talking AT each other. Both are expressing and speaking what they want to say so they can feel better. Neither is actually paying much attention to the other. It is just two people talking at each other, so they can both feel they have been heard. Everyone wants to feel they have been heard. But in reality, neither of them was really heard. However, they both feel some relief because they both got to talk and express what was on their mind. That is not really communicating. That is called talking.

True communication comes when both parties are hearing each other and understanding each other. True communication is when both get to speak and express themselves, and both get to be heard and understood by the other. True communication takes two or more to tango. So, all of you who think you are communicating with your teenager by lecturing them, even though they have their ear-buds in and are just listening to you talk (noise like in Charlie Brown), think again. There is no true communication unless the other person is also able to speak and be heard.

So, I think we have a pretty good handle on Communication. Being a Master Communicator is a little different. It is definitely stepping it up a notch. A Master Communicator is able to skillfully, effectively, and fully express all their thoughts, talking points, and agenda to the other person, with the other person fully understanding and accepting the points you are making. This is really difficult to do. Think about it. It is as if you have this long presentation to make and you need the other person to be fully engaged, understand all you say, and even buy into to what you are saying. Most people have a very short attention span. You usually have several seconds to catch their attention, then maybe a minute to keep their attention, and then you have to be epic to keep their attention for longer periods. We are going to try and figure out how to do this.

As I indicated earlier, it all starts with you LISTENING. You are listening for a few things. You actually have to be paying close attention because there is a lot you need to capture. Firstly, I listen for the person's style of communication. Do they speak in short blurbs? Do they speak in long complex sentences? Do they speak from humor, or being serious? Are they trying to sell you, or convince you, or inform you, or trying just to be heard? Do they have any slight accents, words, or phrases they like to use? Do they speak from high intelligence, or is it more basic?

When I am going to be speaking with someone, I like to LISTEN, LISTEN, LISTEN first. I need to hear from the other person first. I am listening for all the clues and answers to all the questions I raised above. I need to know who I am dealing with. I need to know what language they are speaking. When I say, "what language," I don't mean English or Spanish. I mean that I need to know the STYLE of speaking and communicating. I need to know what language they speak because I am going to speak to them in their own language. What does this mean?

As an example, let's say I listened to you very carefully. Because I am a good listener and I have done this a few times before, I can figure out very quickly your style. I might establish that you speak in short intelligent sentences. You inject humor in your language. You have a habit of looking at the person in the eyes, but then you like to look up at the sky when you are finishing a point. You also like to use the phrase "and that's that" at the end of your speaking paragraphs. I take it all in. What do I do with this information?

I speak in your own language. I am going to try and use your same style of speaking when I communicate with you. I do this because if I speak in your own style of language, you are more likely to listen to me and understand what I am saying to you. You also might start to feel a kinship with me because subconsciously you are noticing that I am just like you, because I speak just like you.

I will be sure to speak in short intelligent sentences. I will add humor along the way. I will even very gently copy a mannerism or two, such as looking up at the sky gently when I am finishing my point. And when I am done speaking, I will signal I have finished by saying "and that's that." You might even laugh when I do this. You might pick up that I am copying you, but you know I am not making fun of you. It is just me trying to bond with you. It is also validation for you that I was paying very close attention to you earlier, such that I picked up your mannerisms and style to speaking. Everyone wants to feel they were listened to and heard, so you will take this as a compliment, and I get points for that. I will have successfully bonded with you and gained your willingness to communicate openly and effectively with me.

So that is the first reason why I am listening very carefully. Rewind and back up, because in reality I still have not spoken to you much. I am still listening. I was listening to figure out your speaking style. I figured that out. But I am still listening because now I need to establish the second big item. I must establish your motive.

Your motive is the reason you are speaking or communicating. You are speaking for a reason. What is that reason? I want to know what you want, or what you need, before I even take my turn to speak. I want to know how you are feeling. Are you sad? Angry? Frustrated? Desperate? What is your mood? Why are you in that mood? What is your current state of mind? What do you need or want most right now? So basically, I am sizing you up to figure out where you are coming from. I WANT to fully understand you. I want to know what you really need or want. Knowing where you are coming from and what you are needing and wanting, allows me to communicate more effectively because I am going to include things relevant to your needs and wants when I speak to you.

I have listened to you. I know how you speak, your style, your sophistication level, and the most effective way for me to bond with you and speak with you more effectively in your own style of language. In addition to all that, I also know your current mood. I know whether I need to be gentle, firm, humorous, serious, highly intelligent, or simple. I also have an idea of what you might be wanting or needing. I have a good feeling for where you are coming from in your communication. I know far more about you than you know about me. Sounds like another advantage, doesn't it?

Finally, it is my turn to speak, and I am ready. As already shown in the earlier scenario, I start to speak to you in your language. But not only that, I also address your mood. I will make a comment about how sorry I am that you are struggling right now. You will take this as validation that again I was listening to you very carefully. Everyone loves to be heard. Then I will quickly throw something into my initial statements about how it sounds like you want or need such-and-such, showing that I was listening so carefully, that I picked up on what is bothering you most at the moment.

I now have your full attention. Between speaking in your own language, proving to you that I care enough to actually fully listen to all you said, by showing concern for your current mood, and finally by mentioning the item that matters to you most now, I now fully have YOUR attention. I have proven to you that I am intelligent enough to listen and understand. I have shown you that I figured out what is bugging you, and you are curious to hear if what I say might include some kind of solution for what you need or want the most. I am also easy to listen to, because I speak in your own language and you like that.

Now that I have your full attention, I can speak and express my points and my own agenda. I am going to speak now, and possibly for a while. So I must keep your attention. I will do this by maintaining a balance. I will balance the task of expressing my own agenda to you, but also inserting tidbits that will be of special interest to you. I will make references to your mood and helping your mood (without being direct). I will make references to possible solutions to your current want or need. In case you forgot, this would be your motive. Your motive is what you want or need. So I will make my points, but also throw you tidbits here and there to keep you engaged and show you that there is plenty in the conversation for you. Eventually, I will have fully expressed myself and my points. I will have done it in a way that kept you engaged and interested. What is the definition of a Master Communicator again? A Master Communicator is able to skillfully, effectively, and fully express all their thoughts, talking points, and agenda to the other person, with the other person fully understanding and accepting the points you are making. Have I been successful in this? Hopefully to some degree. If not, I would keep trying from different angles and directions. Effective communication can be very difficult.

Communication is often most difficult in personal relationships. Here is why. With more formal communication such as above, the conversation is about ideas, facts, and points. When communicating with those we love, the conversation is about FEELINGS. Ideas, facts, and points are often totally irrelevant. It is not WHAT you say. It is HOW you say it that counts more. It is also about LISTENING and UNDERSTANDING, more than speaking.

Being a Master Communicator in personal relationships means LISTENING, then speaking in a way that addresses your partner's FEELINGS. They don't want your facts, ideas, and opinions, as much as they want you to UNDERSTAND HOW THEY ARE FEELING. Do I hear a cheer from you all?? So whether you are a Master Communicator or not, will stem from your ability to fully understand the other person's FEELINGS first. THEN you can speak and express yourself in a way that also addresses the other person's feelings. If the other person is convinced you listened and understand how they are FEELING, they will be many more times likely to listen to YOU. If you miss the mark and don't speak on the level of their feelings, they likely won't even listen to you.

Just a quick example to show how extreme and important this concept is; let us pretend you are desperate to express something to your partner. However, your partner is very upset. How you would want to proceed is by convincing them to speak, while you listen. You will listen, listen, and listen. You will then listen some more. I have seen examples where you will need to listen for an hour before even speaking. You MUST first listen. Then you must convince them you understand their feelings. I do not care if this takes fifteen minutes or five hours. You cannot speak and express YOUR thoughts until you have convinced them that you listened, and that you understand their feelings. Only after those two things can you speak. Then speak. They will listen. How do I know this? Firstly, they will be tired after expressing themselves for a long time. Secondly, they will appreciate that you listened to them and wanted to understand them, so they will give you the small reward of actually listening to YOU. If this doesn't work, then you have bigger problems to deal with than just communication (grin).

Communication and being a Master Communicator is a very difficult skill. It takes lots of practice. But if you can become really good at it, you will find you have a huge advantage in dealing with other people. You will also come out of conversations and presentations as a success more often as you Rise To Greatness.

Chapter Twelve
The Art Of Negotiation

Everything in life is a negotiation. Everything. Many people think negotiation is only for when you are buying a car or house. But in reality, we negotiate every day for everything, including with ourselves. Understanding this is essential and having the ability to negotiate with anyone for anything is an important skill to have. We will go over some of the basics and the different angles and situations in which negotiation is used.

NEGOTIATING WITH PEOPLE

Negotiating with people is a necessary skill and task in order for us to get what we need, what we want, and for what we want to do. We do not live or operate in a vacuum. Fortunately, or unfortunately, we are intertwined with others and depend on them to make our way through life. A person who can't negotiate is a person who is doomed to a life of frustration and being stuck.

When it comes to people who do not possess negotiating skills, there are usually two different groups of people. One type of person simply will not negotiate because they know they can't. This type of person will simply back down, back away, and not even try, if they are confronted with a situation where negotiation is required. This person is very non-confrontational, maybe shy, and likely has had past traumas dealing with people in negotiations.

The second type of person is the "my way or the highway" kind of person. They don't know how to negotiate and are simply not willing to negotiate. They save face by taking a tough stance by refusing any negotiations. This type of person would rather have no deal at all than negotiate. This type of person has been known to cut off their nose to spite their face. Both of these types face frustration, failure, and are missing out on opportunities to progress in life.

It is no accident that the prior chapter was about being a master communicator. You will be using those skills in negotiating. The prior chapters on believing in yourself, motivation, and mastering your emotions also build up to this moment. You have learned many basic skills, and now you are starting to mix them together into new more complex skills. This will be a prime example of that. Well let's get started.

So how do you negotiate with someone? Do you picture an object sitting between you and them, and then you offer low, and they offer high, and you try to meet in the middle? Well, sometimes. But no. Negotiation is not a process. Negotiation is an ART. Negotiation is like a martial art that uses psychology, strategy, and communication skills. You might recognize some of what I am about to say.

The first step in negotiation is to LISTEN. We are under the premise there is something you want from this other person. They

100

have something you want. It could be an object, opportunity, or a certain behavior you want from them. So yes, this other person could even be your child if you want a certain behavior from them. It could be your romantic partner, your boss, or some creepy person on *Craigslist* with something to sell. Whoever it is, you want something from this person.

Regardless of who it is, the first thing I am going to do is LISTEN to them. I want to size them up. I want to figure out their communication style so I can communicate with them in their own language. I want to check their mood and motivation. I want to find any possible advantage I can use during the negotiations. Do they have a cat or dog they are paying too much attention to? You can bet I will be making friends with this cat or dog. I will use any edge or advantage available to me as a negotiator. Making conversation also gives me enough time to learn the person's communication style. I will start to adapt my own speaking style to theirs. They will start to feel more comfortable with me as we bond over similar communication style, and as I comment on things important to them such as their pet. Their guard will come down to some degree. This obviously makes negotiations easier for me and provides me with another advantage.

The next thing I will do is figure out what they want. I cannot emphasis this enough. The most important part of negotiation is figuring out what the other person wants. So many people think negotiation is only about getting what you want. So, people go charging in like a storm trooper trying to get what they want as fast as possible. This is a huge mistake. Doing this causes the other person to raise their guard, and it initiates the ego game of you against them. Once ego gets involved everyone loses. So please don't. Instead, continue remaining mostly silent as you listen. Figure out what the other person wants the most.

We have to dial-in on that statement close-up for a minute. There is what the person SAYS they want, there is what the person REALLY wants, and then there is what the other person NEEDS. You need to identify ALL THREE items. Again, what they say they want, what they really want, and finally what they need.

It is important to identify what they want because a person responds better if you negotiate in terms of what THEY want. Human creatures usually think in terms of themselves. You can use this psychology to your advantage by keeping the person engaged and excited about the negotiation because you are constantly keeping the focus on what THEY want, and this keeps them very interested.

The core secret of negotiation is to give the other person what they REALLY want, or what they NEED, while getting what YOU want in return. All the emphasis so far has been on listening to them, sizing them up, and figuring out what they say they want, really want, and need. Once you have all of that figured out, it's time to make your move. You need to show them how giving you what you want, will give them what they really want or need.

If you have not noticed, you are in total control of the negotiations at this point. You know more about them and their motivations than they know about you. You have listened carefully and know all kinds of things about them, including their wants, needs, and desires. You may have even picked up any vulnerabilities they have. You have taken all this information and have now presented an offer that tempts them with what they truly want and need. Almost unspoken is the fact that you are going to get what YOU want in return.

Notice how I have approached the negotiation from the exact opposite as most people. Instead of charging in with my demands of what I want, I have literally left my own needs for the very end of the process, and nearly unspoken. The other person does not even hear me verbalize what I want until the moment I offer my "suggestion" on how I can GIVE THEM what they want and need. By doing it this way, you have created the appearance of putting the other person first. They will be attracted to this like moths to a flame, and it will also result in good will from them. You have been so nice listening to them, petting their cat, learning about them, and asking about their wants and needs. The least they can do is agree to your terms. By definition, your "terms" will be reasonable because you are giving them what they want. Yes, there might be some back and forth at this point, but it really is just academic, as you will have already won the battle the moment you figured out how to give them what they want while getting what you want.

If there is any difficulty or hang-up in the negotiation, it will be your ability to figure out how to give them what they want while getting what you want. So you need to be clever and intelligent. If you need to have a huddle and think, just be honest with them about that. You can say something like, "I really want to give you what you need, but I have to be able to make this work for me also." This initiates a spirit of cooperation rather than competition. At this point, you might both be working together to come up with a good mutual agreement. This is when you know you are negotiating correctly.

NEGOTIATING WITH LIFE

Remember, when I started this chapter, I said that everything in life is a negotiation. Negotiating does not just apply to people. It applies to life also. A person has to realize that life is a give and take. Many people go through life very frustrated that they are constantly falling short of what they want. We are going through a transformation process in this book in an attempt to help you get more out of life. But still the same, you have to realize you will not get everything you want. Sorry if this violates some Law of Attraction positivity rule of only saying what is wonderful and what you want to hear. Here, let me offer you a tissue to dry your tears.

The reality is that life is tough and even down right brutal. You have to negotiate with it. You have to figure out what you want out of life and figure out what you are willing to give up in order to get it. The reason I am including this topic section is because the thinking is slightly different when negotiating with life. When we negotiate with people, we first find out what they want, and then we figure out how to get what we want by giving them what they want. When negotiating with life, we do it a bit differently.

When negotiating with life we first figure out what WE want. Then we figure out what WE are willing to pay to get it. Everything comes with a price. The price might be incredible effort. The price might be waking up at 5:00AM every morning. The price might be giving up our nights and weekends. The price might be going back to school. The price might be giving up soda and cookies. And yes, the price might also be money. But there is always a price.

What we have above is the makings of a life equation that needs to be balanced. A bit later in the book I will talk about introducing "The Hunter Equation" to help with this life equation. Some of you know what that is already, but I will be explaining in detail, so everyone knows. My point is that life is an equation. It is a balance between what you are willing to give on one side, and what you want to get in return on the other side.

When negotiating with life, you need to first figure out what you want. Then figure out what you are willing to give. The "negotiation" is not one side fighting with the other side. The negotiation is you reconciling the equation so that what you want is equal to what you are willing to give. Doing this will commit you to giving what is required to accomplish your goal. And that my friends, is what this book is about, right? It is about you getting what you want in the end.

NEGOTIATING WITH YOURSELF

Negotiating with yourself is very much you negotiating with life, except you control both sides of the equation. Negotiating with yourself is more about self-respect and self-love. In negotiating with yourself, the thought process is about what you want vs. what you deserve. As in most negotiations, you want the best deal for yourself. You might even want more than what is fair, or you want something for less than what is fair.

The equation of what you want vs. what you deserve is a negotiation with yourself. It is about being honest with yourself. It is a reality check. It is not about arguing with yourself or hating on yourself for your best deal. It is an inner negotiation to reconcile what you want with what you deserve. What do I mean by "what you deserve"? You deserve the best, right? So what am I talking about here? Well, yes, you deserve the best. BUT, I am also helping you become a more amazing person that operates on a higher level of mental integrity. This means owning the fact that you must put out a certain amount to get a certain amount. It is very much related to the negotiation with life.

I felt it important to talk about it here because a big part of this book is the theme of OWNING IT. The negotiation with yourself requires you to own it. It requires you to acknowledge and own the fact that in order to get what you want, you have to deserve it by putting forth the effort in getting it. Again, I apologize if you were expecting this book to tell you that you can have infinite amounts of anything and everything by just thinking a positive happy thought. Here, let me get you another tissue in case I've created more tears.

You know by now this book is about keeping it real and putting forth real work to get real results. There are two sides to every equation, and they must balance out. Just be willing to own the equation and be willing to put out the amount required to receive the amount you want. That is what negotiation is. And it is an art.

Chapter Thirteen
Navigating Toxic People

Okay, strap in, here we go. There is not a living creature on Earth that is immune from toxic people. Of all the tools we are putting in your toolbox, this might be the most important one in terms of protecting your own mental well-being. Toxic people are often the biggest problems we have in our lives. If we did not have many problems before, we have plenty of problems after too much contact with a toxic person. Being with a toxic person is like rolling around in poisonous chemical sludge. It is going to be all over you, and it's going to be in places that are difficult to clean out. But if the toxic sludge is not gross enough, you also end up growing mold all over yourself until you are smothered and can't breathe. Toxic people can squeeze the life out of you like a vampire morphed into a boa constrictor who wrapped around you to squeeze the life out of you, while they sink their fangs into you to suck the remaining life out of you.

Oh my gosh, listen to me. It is as if I have had personal contact and been the victim of toxic people myself. Hmmm. Well DUH! We all have. Therefore, I write this chapter for all of us. Dear lord, save us from the sociopaths and narcissists of the world!

Anyway, I will stop ranting now and get down to business. Your transformation into a greater person would be incomplete and impossible if you do not learn how to deal with toxic people. Since toxic people are the cause of many of our problems, and they often block our progress, it is absolutely essential you learn to deal with them effectively. But I want to stress that I am not offering a cure for dealing with such people. I am only offering some understanding and techniques for managing toxic people so they will not block your progress. Like roaches and weeds, toxic people will still be around no matter what we do. But let's not allow them to affect our lives as much as they have in the past, okay?

We will start by identifying the main types of toxic people. Obviously, first you need to become skilled at identifying such people as quickly as possible, and then classifying them into what type of toxic person they are. Doing this accurately will allow you to deal with them more effectively. After all, we have to first clearly define the problem before we can solve it. So we will work on identifying them first, then come up with solutions, strategies, or coping mechanisms for dealing with them.

SOCIOPATH

There are different official definitions of a Sociopath. It is an actual mental/behavioral disorder. It is associated with the official medical term of ASPD, or Antisocial Personality Disorder. Thus, at its root it is an antisocial disorder. Most people think of Sociopaths as proactively injecting themselves into lives to destroy them. This is true in some ways, but the actual medical disorder is the fact that Sociopaths are unable to function socially in a healthy acceptable way. They do not have normal healthy human traits when it comes to socializing with others. An extroverted person with ASPD will start to exhibit Sociopathic traits in a proactive destructive way, as many of us have seen.

Here are some common traits of a sociopath:

- Lack of Empathy
- Lack of conscience
- Cold/Callous inner being
- Seemingly charming outer shell
- Manipulator
- Lies constantly to the point of believing their own lies.
  Could pass a lie detector test.

I am not going to provide an endless list. Obviously, there are countless traits and symptoms of a sociopath. I want to keep it down to the primary traits, so we do not lose focus. For me personally, I always spot a sociopath by their complete lack of a conscience. This is the telltale sign of a sociopath. They have no conscience because they have no empathy. Due to their antisocial disorder, they are actually incapable of relating to another person on an emotional or empathic level. They do not know how you feel, and they do not care. They only care how THEY feel, and about justifying their own feelings. They will make up any lie in order to justify their own feelings or actions. They will manipulate you without conscience to achieve whatever goal they have in mind. They will do this without any regard for your own feelings or well-being. Remember, they have no conscience.

People often fall into the trap of a sociopath because the sociopath can often be very charming on the surface. If you are a person who has emotional weaknesses and vulnerabilities, a sociopath will seek you out and spot you in a second. They will then charm you and stroke your ego and emotions in order to manipulate their way into your life. Once in your life, they will conduct full-on emotional warfare and take everything they want from you until you are destroyed. If you call them out on this, they will make up countless lies as to why they are doing what they are doing. They will manipulate you more in order to get you to accept their behavior. You might believe their lies because you do not detect any regret or guilt from them, so you assume this means they are telling the truth.

A sociopath is usually very polished, smooth, and good at what they do. They can hide lies in plain sight, and they can be amazingly stealthy about hiding other things you will never find. Their manipulations rolled up in lies that you can never penetrate make them very cunning and hard to deal with. But here is how to deal with a sociopath.

1. Identify them as a Sociopath
2. Block them from entering your inner-self

Some of you will think I am being cheeky or funny with my curt solution. I am not. That is literally how to deal with a sociopath. Let me explain. First off, you cannot fix a sociopath. You cannot cure them. You cannot completely stop them from being who they are. So do not try to conquer them. Secondly, there is no way to totally avoid contact with sociopaths unless you move to a remote island on an iceberg. So, if you cannot avoid them and you cannot fix them or conquer them, what do you do? Just lock them out. That simple.

Here is an example. Let's say you are forced to have contact with a sociopath. You obviously complete step one, which is to clearly identify and label them as a sociopath. So now you know what they are, how they operate, and what you can expect from them. Then in step 2, you lock them out. You block them from entering your inner-self. What I mean by this is that you simply do not buy into any of their nonsense. Whatever they say to you, just nod your head and say, "uh huh." It's that simple. Let's all try it so we know we got it. Ready? Nod your head. Say "uh huh." Awesome, I think you got it. Try it more times if you think you need more practice. But that's it. You do not let them in. Do not believe ANYTHING they say. Do not let their charm engage you. Do not engage with their manipulations. This means do not buy into any compliments they give you since this is normally how it starts. Do not buy into anything.

When you see a sociopath, imagine them as a lion. If you see a lion walking around, do you run up to it and pet it? Do you let it just walk up to you while it licks its lips? No. You walk away. Create distance. If it gets close, you stay silent and make no sudden movements. You just wait for it to leave. So, think of a sociopath in that way. I feel bad for using lions as the example because lions are such beautiful creatures. My apologies. But you get my point. The bottom line is that you are not so much dealing with sociopaths as you are identifying them so that you know to just throw your walls up.

NARCISSIST

Are we having fun yet? Oh, the fun is just beginning, because now we are going to talk about narcissists. Narcissism is technically referred to as NPD, or Narcissistic Personality Disorder. Narcissism is all about having a total focus on your own self-importance. A narcissist literally thinks they are the center of the universe. Only THEY matter, and that is because they are better and more important than you are.

Here are some traits of a narcissist:

- Lack of Empathy
- Exaggerating their own self-importance & superiority
- Consumed with their own appearance, vanity
- Demands constant attention and compliments
- Believe they are more important than you

110

- Believe you and the entire world exist to serve them and all their needs
- Believe they are never wrong, and it is never their fault

The telltale sign of a Narcissist for me is someone who thinks they are the center of the universe and nothing is ever their fault. You will almost never hear a narcissist say, "I'm sorry." You are more likely to find Sasquatch than get an apology from a narcissist. Why? Because a narcissist is never wrong silly. You are the one that is wrong. You owe them an apology. After all, they are more deserving than you are because they are more important than you are. And how dare you be disrespectful by not complimenting them on how wonderful they are 100% of the time. Narcissists are amazing people because they are flawless and wonderful. They can be evil to everyone, but they will still remind you how kind they are to everyone. If only everyone in the world was as perfect as them, the world would be a great place. In a world full of problems (which the narcissist likely created), they will remind you that they are the one person who is not the problem. Everyone else is the problem. How amazing it must be to live in such delusion, yes?

So how does one deal with such a creature? Here is my two-step plan for dealing with a narcissist:

1. Identify the person as a narcissist
2. Never disagree with them.

Okay well that was easy, wasn't it? Let's go over it in more detail though just to make sure. First thing you will do is clearly identify the person as a narcissist. See them for what they are. The second thing you will do is simply never challenge them. Just agree. If a narcissist tells you that the world is flat and they are the most beautiful of them all, just respond by nodding your head and saying, "Okay." Let's all try it. Nod your head. Say, "Okay." Very good. I think you got it.

The trick is to engage with narcissists as little as possible. It can never end well. Therefore, just limit your engagement with them. If they say something ridiculous and insulting just say, "Okay." This lack of challenging them disarms them. A narcissist is used to being challenged so they have their knives and bats handy to attack if needed. So simply do not challenge them. You cannot win. Remember, a narcissist is always right. Plus, even if you won, you would never get an apology anyway, so why bother. Just don't.

GASLIGHTER

Ahhh yes, the Gaslighter. This comes from the term "gas lighting." A Gaslighter is someone who can and will twist anything to their advantage. It does not matter what the subject matter is, a Gaslighter can make it your fault. But a Gaslighter is more than that. A Gaslighter can victimize and damage you, and STILL make it YOUR fault.

Here are some traits of a Gaslighter:

- They accuse you of doing things they themselves did
- They lie
- They deny everything until the end of time
- They harm you and then blame you for it
- They confuse you until you have doubts
- They convince you that you are stupid or crazy even though you are not, and they are

The true sign of a Gaslighter is someone who will victimize you and then blame it on you. A great example of a Gaslighter is someone who cheats on you, but then proceeds to argue that it's your fault they cheated on you. A Gaslighter will twist themselves into a pretzel to confuse you and show in some convoluted way that they were right, and you were wrong. If you call them out on it and prove they were in fact wrong, they will just respond by denying the proven truth and tell you how everything that happens is your fault anyway. A Gaslighter does not believe in reality. If you tell them the world is not flat, they will disagree and accuse you of being too argumentative. Why? Because it's always your fault. Every horrible thing they do to you is always YOUR fault. Whether they cheat on you, lie to you, hurt you, or make a mistake, it will always be your fault they did this. If you challenge them on it, they will have a half dozen tricks up their sleeve to twist it back against you. No matter how horrible a person the Gaslighter is, they will always show you how it is your fault and that you are much more horrible than they are. How do you deal with such ridiculousness? Two step plan:

1. Identify them as a Gaslighter
2. Don't engage

So, when a Gaslighter is gaslighting, just simply recognize it for what it is. Then simply don't engage with it. When I was a kid, someone once told me to never roll in the mud with a pig, because the pig loves it even if I don't. A Gaslighter loves rolling in the mud. So, if you try to engage with them and argue their points with fairness and logic, you will get nowhere, but they will be having a fun time twisting toxicity back at you. Just do not engage in the foolishness.

MENTAL AND PHYSICAL ABUSE

If someone is physically abusive, leave them. They will do it again. They will hurt you, then they will apologize, then they will do again. Rinse and repeat until someone is dead or until you finally leave.

Emotional abuse is common. People are emotionally abusive because of their own issues. It actually has nothing to do with you. The abuser will always blame you and say you "triggered them" and it's your fault for triggering them. Then if they are trying to be honest, they will blame their father or mother for being abusive toward you. But it is usually never their fault where they take full responsibility.

People are abusive toward others usually because others were abusive toward them in the past. Abusers were indeed victims. But it is no excuse for them victimizing others. The only cure is for the chain of abuse to be broken. There are two ways to do this as far as your involvement is concerned. The first way is for you to just leave them and stop all contact. That fixes it. But the other way is for the abuser to go into counseling and work on themselves. Abusers can be fixed in the sense that if they take full responsibility for their behavior AND go into counseling to root out the cause of their behavior, they can improve with time. People are not born Abusers. They were abused in order to become abusers. So that needs to be identified, isolated, and rooted out. Entire books are written on this.

BULLY

A bully is a jerk who takes out his own insecurities on those he thinks are weaker than him. A bully is not mean because they were born that way. A bully is mean because they are suffering from some issue within themselves. Bullies are often people who were bullied themselves. Bullies are often victims of abuse. The bully takes out their own frustrations and issues on others by treating them in horrible ways, as they themselves have been treated.

The one true mark of a bully is that a bully is always weak inside. Whereas a sociopath or narcissist has the strength of a nuclear arsenal, a bully is nothing but a thin tough exterior covering a fragile weak inner core. Bullies are usually cowards. If they are challenged correctly, they will find a way to save face, back down, and find an easier target.

Therefore, the best way to deal with a bully is to first try avoiding them or diverting attention away to some shiny object in the distance (bullies are not very smart). But if a confrontation is inevitable, the best thing you can do is stand up straight and confront them head-on.

A bully fears a strong opponent. If you can appear strong and vicious to them, they will immediately try and find a way to evacuate themselves. Thus, even smarter would be if you "give them an out."

What I used to do with bullies is I would stand up to them. I would show them I was ready to go head-to-head. Then out of the blue I would say, "You are probably stronger and smarter than me." They would use this as their "out" to back away. This allowed them to "save face" and still feel superior but allow them to back off without confronting me further, because the truth is that they realized they no longer wanted to confront me when they saw I was willing to stand up to them. They just needed that "out" so they would not look weak and stupid. Stand up to them with ALL YOUR FORCE, then give them something that makes them think they have won so they can back away. They are not very smart, so some basic psychology tricks work.

BLUFF BULLY

A bluff bully is even more pathetic than a common bully. A bluff bully is one of these gruff people who bark but have no bite. Not only do they not bite, but often they don't even have any teeth. It is as if they are barking in some delusional way to convince themselves they have power, when in fact they have no power. Bluff bullies are these people you meet who just want to be contrarians. They disagree with everything you say just so they can disagree.

You might say something, and the bluff bully in a loud menacing voice will say, "YOU ARE STUPID, you should go back to school," then they will usually follow that up by laughing as loud as possible. But in truth, they are always the stupid ones. That is why they are bluff bullies. They are engaging in a desperate attempt to make themselves feel smarter and better, even though they know they are pathetic.

Best way to deal with a bluff bully is to just stare at them. They are not even worth engaging with. That is how pathetic they are. When they are reminded of how pathetic they are by your non-response, because they are too stupid for your time, they will slink off and not bother you.

TROLLS AND IGNORANTS

Trolls and what I call "Ignorants" are just people who enjoy spreading misery as their hobby. These people are miserable themselves. They find some solace in spreading their misery around. These people are a step down from bullies because they usually won't engage face to face. They usually will only engage online, or notes, or messages. They wouldn't dare troll you to your face. These people often act normally in person. The Troll in them only comes out in the semi-anonymity of online social media.

They just want to make the rest of the world as miserable as they are. Often, they like to disagree even if they agree. They only want to cause frustration and try to drag people down to their level. There is no substance to their behavior and as I said, they often only do this part-time. Get a life I say.

MIXTURES

Keep in mind that any and all of the above toxic types can be combined and mixed together for special blends of gross toxicity. For example, you can commonly face a sociopathic narcissist or a narcissistic sociopath. As the titles would indicate, this is when both types of toxicity are combined.

My personal favorite is a gaslighting narcissistic sociopath. These awful creatures are interesting to observe. They are clear sociopaths, totally delusional with no conscience, who think they are the center of the universe and everyone is wrong about them. They will twist everything back at you to prove they are always right, and everything is always your fault. Such a person is constantly telling everyone how wonderful and amazing they are, while victimizing and hurting people, but instantaneously blaming their own hurtful actions on their victims. I think we have all seen this in action, haven't we? Toxicity at its best.

ARE YOU A TOXIC PERSON?

So, are you? I would be remiss if I did not ask this horrible question. You know by now that I am all about keeping it real. So if we are to keep it real, we must admit and accept the fact that some of us have some of these toxic features within ourselves, or did at one time perhaps. That does not mean we are horrible people. Keep in mind that most of these behaviors exist on a sliding scale, so that some of us might have a couple of the traits of one, but not all of the traits, or some traits in very small degrees.

I am constantly checking myself on my own behavior in all realms of life. I would suggest you all do the same. None of us are perfect. We are all flawed in some way, and we are all learning and growing. Those of us who inspect ourselves objectively and own up to our faults and baggage, tend to grow and evolve faster. So own your stuff. Admit and acknowledge any shortcomings to yourself. Then work to improve them.

What I am gently saying is that if you recognize any of the above behaviors in yourself, don't condemn yourself as a hopelessly toxic person. Instead, take a very quick visit back to Chapter 2 on *Wiping The Slate Clean*, and take out more garbage and debris. Perhaps you did not fully recognize some behaviors as garbage that needs to be removed. Fair enough. But remove it now. This is a work in progress. Nobody said it was going to be pretty. Some of you by now have gone back to past chapters more than once. This is supposed to be messy. The only thing that matters is that you finish successfully. So, take your time, go back, and make corrections as often as you need. The self-awareness of you checking yourself and making corrections is a sure sign that you are indeed Rising To Greatness.

Chapter Fourteen
Exploiting Opportunity

Every good Jedi knows how to search for opportunity, know an opportunity when they see it, and then exploit it to their optimal benefit. An even more clever Jedi knows how to turn almost any situation into an opportunity. Thus, we definitely have to explore this concept.

There are a couple different ways to find opportunity. The first is to go looking for it. The second is to let it find you. But there is a third way that is my favorite. The third is to take normal or bad situations that are sitting at your feet and turn them into opportunities. In this chapter, I will go through different ways and scenarios that you can exploit opportunities.

However, before we start going opportunity hunting, we have to make sure we are prepared. There are a couple things you must do in order to be ready for opportunities. First, you have to think with your intellectual brain instead of your emotions. Anytime a person is thinking with their emotions, they are pretty much blind and dumb. Emotions have a way of making us only see two inches in front of our nose; and sometimes we only see what we want to see, or what we *think* we see, rather than what is really there. Additionally, thinking with emotions often results in making poor decisions. The chapter on mastering your emotions really comes into play here.

When you are on the lookout for opportunity, you need to set aside your emotions and be in total "intellectual brain thinking mode." Looking for opportunities is very similar to hunting for food when alone in the wilderness. There are times we NEED an opportunity. It might be a job, a gig, a contract, or even that perfect apartment, house, or car. You are looking for something because you need it or want it. You are hungry. So you need to go hunting for food. When you are alone and hungry in the wilderness, and hunting for food, it's GAME ON. You have to be clear-minded and serious. You have to be aware of all your surroundings and what is going on around you. You have to always be aware, thinking, and ready. Sorry to those offended by hunting, but that is what humans used to do eons ago to survive, so the analogy fits. So, when you are hungry for an opportunity and need to go hunting for one, you need to be in the same frame of mind. GAME ON.

The second thing you need to have prepared is a mental inventory of your skill sets, and all your available resources you have to offer. If we have no money, but are out searching to get what we need, we have to be willing and able to barter for what we want or need. When a person sets out to barter for what they want, they already know what they have available to trade. When searching for opportunities, you must always know ahead of time what you have to trade, give, sell, and offer in return for engaging with a desired opportunity. In these times, and in the context of this book, this means you need an inventory of your skills, abilities, and resources. You need to be fully aware of everything you have to offer someone. We already worked on this in previous chapters, including developing a sense of self, where we made various lists and inventories. Don't you just love how all the work we already did is coming into full use, and being combined with all other skills?

Be sure you have an inventory in your head of possible skills, abilities, and resources you have to offer for any opportunities that may arise. The reason you need to be ready is because opportunities often have a short window in which to act upon them or take advantage. There is often no time to leave, think, and come back later. When they used to hunt to stay alive, they did not see their prey, and just return to their village and contemplate whether to take it or not. When you see it, you usually have to take it right then and there. Most of us who went car shopping for our first junker used car when we were teenagers, have experienced the frustration of finding a car we loved, but we had to go home and talk to our parents and see if we could gather the money, only to find out someone bought the car out from under us before we could go back and buy it. We lost out because we did not seal the deal when we had the chance. For our purposes here, we really need to be ready to seal the deal on any opportunity that arises, when it arises. You snooze, you lose. Now that we are fully prepared to be on top of our game and immediately pounce on any opportunities, let's move forward in finding them.

ALWAYS GIVE OTHERS WHAT THEY WANT

Wait, does that title above say for you to always be looking to give others what they are wanting? Does that title almost suggest that you are going out into the world looking for ways to give OTHERS opportunities? I thought the whole idea was for you to find opportunities for yourself. Well I can tell you that the section title above is not a typo. In fact, the best way for you to find opportunities is to actually figure out ways to give other people what they want. You should recognize this technique from our chapter on The Art Of Negotiation. Remember when we talked about giving the other person what they want or need in order to get what we want? Same situation here. Let me give you an example.

You are jobless and actively looking for opportunities. You are meeting your friend at her workplace so you both can go out to lunch on her lunch break. You walk into her place of work and see a person (your friend's boss) complaining that he has no time because he spends all his time trying to figure out his inventory, tasks lists, and so on and so forth. You spot an opportunity because you know that on your own list of skills and abilities, you are an expert at spreadsheets and tracking inventories of things. So you say to your friend's boss, "It sounds like you need an expert on spreadsheets and someone who can efficiently track your inventory and tasks." The boss says, "Yes very badly." You say, "I have a lot of experience doing that. What kind of inventories and tasks do you need to track"? Now you are engaging in a conversation talking business. At the right moment you close the deal and say, "I happen to be looking for an opportunity to help someone do exactly what you need. Would you be interested in having me help you out for a couple days, and then if it is working for you, maybe we talk more?"

What happened above is you were not intending on coming across an opportunity right then. You intended on only meeting your friend for lunch. But you were on your game, always looking, and always prepared. You saw a need someone else had, and knew you could give that person what they wanted. You considered your own inventory of skills and knew you had the ability to give this person what they needed. You engaged in effective communication and negotiation to rope them into giving you a trial run. This is how it's done, because in reality this boss was not looking for a new employee, nor would he ever entertain interviews or trials. But you opened up an opportunity for yourself and wormed your way into a situation that sold him into giving you a try, and possibly giving you a job. During the trial run, you would further seal the deal by making his life as easy as possible.

He will love it and will not want to go back to his old life of horror. Even though there is no money in the budget for a new employee, he will find the money to keep you on because it is making his life so much easier. Good job exploiting that opportunity!

You hopefully see how this is done. Just like with negotiation, you are not pushing yourself on others to get opportunities. The real effective art of opportunity is to see a need or weakness another person has, and then show them you can solve their problem and give them what they want and need. By giving them what they want, you will have an opportunity for yourself. After your foot is in the door, you can mold and stretch the opportunity to better fit YOUR wants and needs. But first make sure the other person is getting everything they want and need. You see by now that most things in life work better if you give the other person what they want first, then afterward you can more easily get what you want from them, and more.

MAKE LEMONADE OUT OF LEMONS

Making lemonade out of lemons is all about taking a bad situation and turning it into an opportunity. In order to do this effectively, you must have taken seriously what I said about setting aside your emotions and instead thinking with your brain. Whenever you find yourself in a bad situation where things have gone wrong, your first thought should be, "I wonder if can somehow turn this into an opportunity." If you start thinking that way instead of just being upset and having a tantrum, you will be surprised at how often you can turn bad things into good opportunities.

The best way for me to demonstrate this is to tell a story that a friend of mine told me of what happened to him one day. He was at a pizza place and ordered his pizza at the counter. He took his drink and went to sit down and wait for his pizza to come out. The only problem is that the pizza never came out. He noticed people who ordered after him had already gotten their pizza, so we went up to the counter to ask about his pizza. Obviously, anyone in his position would be annoyed at this point. He asked about his pizza and it became immediately clear that they had somehow lost his order and his pizza was never made.

At this point in the story, most people would have become very annoyed and angry. Some would have raised their voices and lashed out. Others would have just walked out in retaliation and disgust. But my friend is smart, and he calmly told the manager how he was looking forward to enjoying his pizza at their restaurant, and it would be a huge disappointment for this situation to become his memory and lasting review of the establishment.

The manager caught on fast and wanted to make it right. My friend was not yelling, insulting, or threatening the manager. My friend was using his intellectual brain to engage in the most beneficial way. There may have been some mention about how he would stay and give the place a go if they brought his pizza out free of charge when it was done. The manager immediately offered to get his pizza made immediately and it would be free. Not only that, but his drink was free, and he would be receiving a coupon for a free pizza for his next visit.

My friend had a bad situation that would have angered all of us. We are sitting and waiting for our pizza and it never comes because some idiot lost our order. Just our crappy luck, right? BUT we keep our emotions and tantrums to ourselves. Instead, be smart and find a way to turn the bad situation into an opportunity. Two free pizzas sound good to me. Nicely played.

You can use this strategy in any situation. When someone screws up or harms you, the first thing you think of should be "How can I turn this into an opportunity?" Do not get mad and fly off the handle. Instead, convert the bad event into an opportunity. For those of us who have bad things happen to us all the time, this means you have many possible opportunities being thrown at you all the time. Learn to love those lemons.

ONE PERSON'S JUNK IS ANOTHER'S TREASURE

Many times we are presented with opportunities that do not look that great. We can see that others have already turned it down. Why would you want an opportunity that many others have already turned down? Simple. If you are smarter and more clever than the others, you can find a way to make this junky opportunity shine.

I used to be involved in a company that provided cleaning and maintenance services to office buildings. There was this one time that a bank wanted us to handle the cleaning for this small branch office they had out in the middle of nowhere. They offered it to us because nobody else wanted to do it. It would not be profitable to take on this building, so everyone just turned them down without hesitation. Except me. What I did is I looked at this "junky" opportunity and I found a way to put some shine on it. I suggested that we could take on this building if they also gave us their other remote buildings nobody wanted. They paused wondering why I would want all the remote buildings when nobody even wanted one building. Of course, what I determined is that if I had several of these buildings, I could have a full-time person taking care of all of them and could actually make a profitable venture out of it. They agreed, and we ended up with a large contract of numerous remote buildings. The large bulk of business worked out fine for us, even though it was remote. Plus, we started getting contracts at the prime locations all our competitors wanted. I took junk that nobody else wanted and turned down, and I made it into a treasure for myself. So when you see junk, look at it carefully. Look all around it. Look at what it's connected to and different ways it could be used. Very often junk can be put to good use and it is a cheap opportunity waiting to be exploited.

DIAMOND IN THE ROUGH

Sometimes there is a quality opportunity available, but there is something wrong with it and others pass it by because people are always looking for something that is perfect and easy. Mistake.

Best example of this is a store I knew of that would buy high quality "scratch and dent" items. There would be high-end quality appliances, but there would literally be some scratch or dent, or something wrong. They would buy these damaged items from the large stores for next to nothing, since the large stores considered them junk and unsalable. This "scratch and dent store" would then buff out scratches, conceal or fix dents in clever ways, use touch up paint, and so forth, reconditioning the items to 99% perfect. They could then sell them for 80% of full retail, which was a deal for the customers who saw nothing wrong with the items, but was a huge profit for the store who bought the items at only 10% of retail.

People very often pass by great opportunities because something is not right. Instead, ask yourself "How can I fix this opportunity or make it right"? If it is a job or some kind of business opportunity, you can even suggest to the boss a way to make the job palatable, or the opportunity desirable, and you would be highly interested in working with them to do this. You always have to be willing to look outside the box and get your hands dirty.

I suppose an entire book could be written just on finding and taking advantage of opportunities. My only aim in this brief look was to open your mind to always be searching for, identifying, and taking full advantage of any opportunities that come your way. Part of your Rise To Greatness is all about getting more opportunities so that you can live a better life doing what you want to do.

Chapter Fifteen
Applying
The Hunter Equation

Those of you who have read *The Hunter Equation* know what the Hunter Equation is. Feel free to skip through this chapter but stick with us if you feel a refresher would be helpful. For those of you who did not read the book *The Hunter Equation*, I need to explain to you what the actual Hunter Equation is. I am no longer talking about the book. I am talking about the actual Universal life equation called the Hunter Equation.

The Hunter Equation is a life equation that came through to me from the powers of the Universe after years of frustration over The Law of Attraction. I was never a fan of The Law of Attraction because I recognized early on that The Law of Attraction was flawed and incomplete. The Law of Attraction indicates that your thoughts bring you your results. Meaning, if you think positive thoughts, you will receive positive life results. Millions of people embraced this theory because their positive thoughts made them feel better and seemed to bring them more positive results in their life.

I obviously have nothing against people feeling better and receiving better results in their life. But I felt most of the hype was just based on the positive results side and ignored the negative results side. Basically, people would give Law of Attraction credit when they received good results, but never said anything if it did not work out. Also, I knew that having positive intents and taking positive actions, was not enough to yield positive results in your life consistently.

The Law of Attraction also warns that if you have negative thoughts or intents, negative things will come into your life. A few things bothered me about this. I felt it was a bit narcissistic and gaslighting because The Law of Attraction essentially blames you if bad things happen to you. The Law of Attraction indicates you must have had a negative thought that brought you a negative result. I raise the example of children who get cancer. Did these innocent children have a negative thought that resulted in them getting cancer? Are the children to blame for their own cancer? Of course not! Law of Attraction proponents would say that children getting cancer has nothing to do with Law of Attraction. They might even say that most of the bad things that happen to you, have nothing to do with Law of Attraction. My argument is that if this is the case, then are they claiming that The Law of Attraction only works for positive things and not negative things? Is the Universe only one way? Does only good exist and bad does not? Does only light exist, and dark does not? Do life equations only have one side to them? Do we get to pick and choose what we believe, and just disregard all other truths, simply because we don't like them? So if I think a happy thought and something good happens, it is Law of Attraction in motion? And if I think a bad thought and something bad happens, it is Law of Attraction in motion? But if horrible things happen to good people with good thoughts, we will just ignore that and pretend it does not exist? Also, when horrible people with horrible thoughts have great fortune happen to them, we will pretend that does not exist as well? Are we that unsophisticated and shallow? Do some only wear rose-colored glasses and pretend that is reality? Yep, they do. Good for them. I am not here to tear down others or destroy The Law of Attraction. I am here to explain how The Law of Attraction is incomplete and does not reflect reality. I believe I received the complete life equation from the Universe that some would say completes the Law of Attraction.

For our purposes here, let's say the Law of Attraction is BASICALLY saying that your OUTCOME is equal to your THOUGHTS/INTENT plus your ACTIONS. I know people have different views of the Law of Attraction and some would want to wrestle me in the weeds and parse words over it. But the above statement is an accurate BASIC understanding of the Law of Attraction. Based on the above statement, the Law of Attraction is based on two elements. Your Outcome = Intent + Actions.

The Hunter Equation adds additional elements to the equation. The Hunter Equation states:

FUTURE OUTCOME =
INTENT + ACTIONS + EXTERNAL FORCES + RANDOM LUCK

The Hunter Equation adds the additional elements of External Forces and Random Luck to the life equation. For clarity sake, I am going explain each of the elements, so we are very clear on how this equation works.

FUTURE OUTCOME - Your FUTURE OUTCOME is obviously your results. It can also be your goal. So if you had a goal you were trying to reach or achieve, you would put the goal or desired outcome into the equation as the Future Outcome. The Future Outcome can also be the unintended result of what you received.

INTENT - The INTENT is your intention and attitude. If you understand the Law of Attraction, then you understand what the Intent is. Intent means the same here as it does with the Law of Attraction. Intent is what you are intending and your attitude toward your intention.

ACTIONS - The ACTIONS are exactly what you think they are. These are the steps or actions you are taking. Actions can be positive, negative, or neutral. Actions are simply what you are doing.

EXTERNAL FORCES - This is the first new element I introduced, and likely the most important. EXTERNAL FORCES are all the things that can happen outside of your control. We do not control External Forces. We do not live in a vacuum, and sometimes things surrounding us affect us. Sometimes it does not matter how positive your thoughts and attitudes are, bad things can still happen, or we get results we did not anticipate. An example of an External Force would be when we are doing a great job at work, the boss loves us, we have a great attitude, great thoughts, and everything is going great; but then the company gets bought out and you get fired because of the restructuring. That is an External Force. You have no control over it, and there is nothing you could have done to avoid it. Life happens. Conversely, your boss giving you an unexpected raise can also be an External Force because it was mostly out of your control and not anticipated, yet it will have a major impact on your situation.

Health issues outside our control are other External Force. Things that happen to our family members that change our lives are External Forces. So much of life is a result of External Forces. It does not matter how great your thoughts and attitudes are. THIS is the reason I think Law of Attraction can be a bit narcissistic or gaslight you. Law of Attraction might say that you somehow could have avoided bad things happening to you if you had a more positive outlook, thoughts, intentions, or what have you. But we can clearly see there are plenty of instances where bad things happen completely outside our control, regardless of how positive our thoughts were. Basically, the Law of Attraction will blame you for your misfortune, saying it's your fault because of your thoughts, or even actions. Sometimes, things that happen to us are NOT our fault. Tell that to soldiers who get their leg blown off. Tell that to the kids who gets cancer. MANY things are NOT in our control. Our thoughts are irrelevant in many cases. External Forces take this Universal truth and reality into account. Any life theory that does not account for External Forces outside our control is simply not based in reality.

RANDOM LUCK - This is the second element I added. RANDOM LUCK is controversial because some people do not believe anything is random. Some people believe there is a reason for everything, and everything is based on your destiny and pre-ordained design. I disagree fully. I believe that there is a random element in the Universe. If you put a bunch of jellybeans in a jar, close your eyes, reach in, and pull one out, was that jellybean randomly chosen, or was it pre-ordained that it would be chosen? Yes, some of you will argue with me until the end of time that the one jellybean you chose was meant to be chosen from the beginning of its existence. We will have to agree to disagree. Do you also believe every time you throw dice, that the outcome is pre-ordained? Do you also believe the world is flat? From a scientific point of view, I believe there is a random component because the Universe is always expanding, black holes changing, things growing, things dying, things being born. All these organic changes ensure there are constant VARIATIONS and VARIABLES in the Universe. These variables allow a random component to exist. But back down here to our reality, it just makes sense that some things are random. To be honest, I explain all of this in much more detail and in-depth in *The Hunter Equation* book. But I am hoping I have adequately made my case so you will at least accept the possibility of a random component so that we can move forward with the equation. In summary, Random Luck is that element that not only do we not control it, but nobody controls it.

That is the Hunter Equation. Now let's get back to Rising To Greatness and how we can use the Hunter Equation to our benefit. We use the Hunter Equation to help us set goals, analyze outcomes, contingency plans, anticipate possible external forces, and to make choices in an orderly logical way. I am introducing the equation at this point in the book because we are about to get into such topics as solving problems and making decisions. The Hunter Equation is a useful tool for problem solving and decision making, so it's helpful for you to understand how to use it before we move further. Without further ado, let's go through an example of how to apply the Hunter Equation.

Assume you want to start your own business. As you set this goal, create your plan, and prepare to take the leap, you might want to engage the Hunter Equation first. As a reminder, the Hunter Equation is:

FUTURE OUTCOME =
INTENT + ACTIONS + EXTERNAL FORCES + RANDOM LUCK

So let's start filling in the equation. The **FUTURE OUTCOME** is your goal. So the Future Outcome will be "Your New Business." This will hopefully be the desired end-result of all your efforts.

The **INTENT** is going to be your very positive thoughts and intention for this new business. Your Intent might include the fact you are doing this new business to help other people and make their lives better and easier. Your Intent would include your desire to provide excellent customer service. The Intent would include your intention of loving what you do and enjoying your work. The Intent is all the love and passion you have. The Intent needs to be positive obviously.

The **ACTIONS** are all of the steps required to make this business happen. The Actions will basically be your business plan. The Actions will be your step-by-step plan and task list. An important note is that the Actions element itself is also subject to the entire Hunter Equation.

What I mean by that is when we look at the Actions, you need to also have the correct positive Intent toward the Actions. You also need to keep in mind the Actions are subject to External Forces hitting them, as well as Random Luck.

The **EXTERNAL FORCES** in this case will be all the possible things that can go wrong or go right. The External Forces portion is where you sit down and ANTICIPATE any and all possible things that can happen. Examples might be like "what if the bank does not support me," "what if the similar business to mine across town decides to attack me," "what if my sales are slower than I expect," "what if business is so amazing that I can't keep up," etc. The External Forces is your time to consider all possible weird things that can happen and start planning what your contingency plans will be.

CONTINGENCY PLANS are critical in anything you do in life. You must expect anything and plan for anything. Do not be scared, be ready. Examining the External Forces up front provides you an opportunity to give your plans more in-depth thought, and at least have some back-up plans formulated. Looking at External Forces will also flush out some flaws in your plan so that you can make adjustments before you encounter the problem.

Next, you will consider the **RANDOM LUCK** factor. Good luck and bad luck both exist. Things might go better than expected. Great. Things also might go worse than expected. Be prepared. The Random Luck factor keeps you grounded in reality. How many people have you seen had their head in the clouds about something, and then got wiped out because something went wrong? Considering the Random Luck factor in your equation keeps you realistic and aware that something totally weird and unexpected might happen, and that you need to be ready and willing to accept and deal with such an eventuality.

That's your equation filled out, but you are not done yet. Now you can use the equation to try and improve your situation and chances for success. For example, you will examine EACH OF YOUR ACTIONS, and see how much any of those Actions are vulnerable to

External Forces or bad Luck. If you find Actions that are super vulnerable or have a high likelihood of having negative External Forces or bad luck, you might want to consider altering those Actions so they are less vulnerable. Additionally, you can look at the possible External Factors you listed and see if some of those External Factors can be AVOIDED UP FRONT by taking certain other Actions before you start. This is where looking ahead helps you anticipate certain things and improve your chances. You can also look at your Random Luck element. Is there some possible item of bad luck you are afraid might happen? If so, are there any Actions you can take to lessen the chances of bad luck, or increase the probability of good luck? Furthermore, are there any possible GOOD External Factors you can proactively engage with to help your situation? For example, maybe you know a friend who can provide a very good recommendation or referral for you. The friend doing that would be an External Factor (since it is outside your control), and that External Force would be very positive for you.

I do not want to get you totally lost in a maze of weeds. I could go on for days doing this, twisting and turning, and going backwards and forwards with this equation. I am hoping you are seeing how that is done, and you can realize how to do it. Going up and down the equation, forwards and backwards, is a great way to flush out flaws in your plan, and to add things that will improve your plan.

The Hunter Equation can also be used for personal relationships and personal issues. For example, let's say you want to lose weight. The Future Outcome would be "lose 20 pounds." The Intent would be your positive intentions for becoming healthier, feeling better, living better, and just being happier and more positive. You would be excited and enthusiastic about your intention for this goal. The Actions will be your exact plan of action of how you will lose the weight, such as a certain diet and exercise program. The External Forces will be the possible problems to crop up such as going to a party where there is the best-looking cake ever. What is your contingency plan if you find yourself in such a difficult tempting situation? Make sure you take into account these External Forces and have a contingency plan or coping mechanism in place to deal with it up front. Also, realize that Random Luck could dish out some bad luck at any time. For example, maybe you sustain an injury that will halt your exercise program. What then? Realize this is possible and perhaps give greater caution to lessen the chances of you getting injured, but also accept it could happen, and have a contingency plan in place if it does happen.

Again, I could go on for days and pages with examples, but we have to keep it moving. You are busy and on a mission. But know that the Hunter Equation can be used for most everything in your life. It is helpful in organizing your thoughts, anticipating issues, making contingency plans, and increasing your chances of success. This is why applying the Hunter Equation is a helpful tool in your Rise To Greatness.

Chapter Sixteen
Decision Maker

Having the ability to make quick and good decisions is an important part of being a successful empowered person. If you are not able to make decisions, you end up putting things off, wobbling around, and letting the world choose for you. Quite often, you will be very unhappy with what the world has chosen for you.

Many people seem unable or unwilling to make decisions for a variety of reasons. Some are unable to clearly define their options, are unable to analyze the pluses and minuses of each choice, and others are afraid of making the wrong choice, so they make no choice at all. But usually making no choice at all produces an unfavorable return.

On the contrary, those who are very effective at making decisions, tend to be much more productive, successful, and have a greater amount of control over their lives and destiny. By "success" I don't mean all their decisions are always correct. In fact, some of their decisions will be incorrect. But good decision makers are able to make new decisions that allow them to move on from setbacks quickly. It is better to make many decisions quickly as needed and have some of them wrong, than it is to be paralyzed by not making any decisions at all. With that said, it is obviously better if we can make more good decisions than bad decisions. We will endeavor to increase your chances of making more good decisions, and have you make them quickly and often.

Let's start by breaking down the basic steps in decision making:
1. Clearly define all the available choices
2. Create a pros and cons list for each choice
3. Test drive your choices inside the Hunter Equation
4. Refine and adjust your choices
5. Choose and Execute

1. Clearly define all the available choices

The most important part of decision-making is making sure you have all the best choices in front of you. The biggest mistake people make in decision-making is missing a great choice. Any delay in your decision-making process should only be due to this first step in the process. You want to be certain you have all the best choices in front of you. This is a good time to confirm you have a clear understanding of the available choices, make phone calls, do some checking, and asking for advice. Having a clear understanding of all the choices in front of you can make or break your final outcome.

2. Create a pros and cons list for each choice

Your next step will be to take each choice and create a pros and cons list. By now, you know how much I love making lists. Lots of lists.

Clarity and organization are keys to success. So, take each choice and make a list of all reasons the choice is favorable to you, and make a separate list of all reasons the choice is bad for you. You want to double check to be sure you have thought of all possible pros and cons, because forgetting a big important con can really throw off your final results.

3. Test drive your choices inside the Hunter Equation

Now that you have the Hunter Equation in your toolbox, you might find that you use it often. Making decisions is a great way to use it. Again, a reminder, the **Hunter Equation** is:

Future Outcome =
Intent + Actions + External Forces + Random Luck

Here is how you test drive each choice using the equation. First, you plug your goal or desired outcome into the Future Outcome element. Obviously, your goal/desired outcome/Future Outcome needs to be relevant to the choice you are trying to make. Next, plug each choice (one at a time) into the ACTIONS element. Then run the equation. Knowing what Future Outcome you want, taking into account the Intent you are employing, and now using your CHOICE in the ACTIONS element, look at what possible External Forces that particular choice might trigger, and also look at what kind of Random Luck factor is involved with that particular choice. Is this particular choice more or less vulnerable to bad luck? Does this particular choice trigger more possible External Forces that might complicate things, or does it actually cause the External Forces to be more neutral or in your favor?

Basically, you are trying to determine if this choice is favorable or unfavorable to the possible External Forces and Luck, compared to all the other choices. You want to run each choice through the equation individually. Running the choices through the Hunter Equation is a way of adding to your pros and cons list. For example, if after running a choice through the equation, you determine that it might trigger all kinds of External Forces that might hang things up for you, then you will actually write in your "cons list" something like, "many possible negative External Forces." Or you might write something like, "higher likelihood of being hit with bad luck." Of course, you might see good news from the equation, and if so, you will add those thoughts to your "pros list." Your goal is to gain as much accurate clarity as possible.

4. Refine and adjust your choices

After you run each choice through the Hunter Equation, and you have a good solid list of pros and cons, you might be able to eliminate some choices, and change others. Using a process of elimination to narrow down your choices can be very helpful. But what I am hoping is that after all your above analysis, you might conclude you can modify, bend, or create new choices based on any ideas you may have come up with during the analysis process. This step in the process is your chance to narrow down the choices and adjust all final choices available.

5. Choose and Execute

You have your final choices in front of you. You have good clarity on each choice. You have the pros and cons of each choice. The choices have been tested in the Hunter Equation. Now it's just a matter of judging which choice is the most beneficial to you, and the least potentially harmful to you. Make your pick. Grab it. Embrace it. Own it. Proceed with it.

The process above does not guarantee your decision will always be correct or your choices will be great. You will still make mistakes and bad decisions. What the process above does is give you a solid method of making sound decisions. You can have confidence that you did everything possible to make the best decision, given the information at the time. Having this comfort actually makes it easier to accept the outcome of your decisions. If a decision goes bad, you can at least tell yourself that you made the best choice at the time and you would likely make the same choice again, given the same information.

Making perfect decisions all the time is impossible. You can only work with what you are in control of at the time. You are not responsible for things outside your control. So, make sure your focus is primarily on what is within your control. The first thing that is in your control is your power to immediately face your decisions, consider them carefully and responsibly, and then make the best possible decision without delay. This is the efficient and responsible thing to do. You can always make changes as circumstances change and you start to receive outcome results from your decisions.

Like everything else in this book, the aim is to face your decisions head on, get full clarity, use all your resources to analyze your choices, and then make the best possible decision regarding your desired outcome. You are a Decision Maker.

Chapter Seventeen
Problem Solver

This chapter is quite similar to the chapter you just read on being a decision maker. Obviously, solving problems is about coming up with choices and making decisions. I thought of combining the chapters but realized that the ability to solve problems is too important and deserves its own chapter. Thus, forgive me if this process is similar to the prior chapter. I will just come right out with it. What makes solving problems any different from making decisions? The answer is that problems are far more difficult than decisions, because decisions tend to be black and white choices that we must choose. Solving problems is all about coming up with a SOLUTION, which is often complicated, difficult, convoluted, and has many grey areas.

There is yet another reason why solving problems is more difficult than making decisions. For the most part, people seem to have an easier time choosing from choices and making a decision. However, people hate, and avoid, solving problems. People hate and avoid problems, period. Some people specialize in avoiding their problems. In order to Rise To Greatness, you MUST be proficient at solving problems. Life is full of problems. Sometimes it seems all we get are problems every single day and all day long. Problems are like air. We breathe it, walk in it, live in it, and problems surround us everywhere we go. Thus, avoiding problems is impossible, and trying to do so will always yield a negative outcome.

Therefore, the first step in solving problems is to face your problems head on. There is just no point in avoiding your problems. In fact, I suggest the opposite approach. This advice comes from me personally from my own experience. Believe me, I have tried dealing with problems all different ways. I have tried avoiding them, ignoring them, fighting them, being beaten by them, running from them, running to them, and solving them. I've done it all. I can tell you that the most effective approach for me has been to LEAN INTO THE PROBLEM.

When you see the problem coming, or see it at your doorstep, you want to LEAN INTO IT. That means anticipate it if possible, and not only face it, but face it with enthusiasm and force. Let me give you another one of my analogies.

Let's say you are inside your little house. You know a mean man is coming to your door to be mean to you. Many of us might just lock the doors and hide in the corner, cowering in fear while the mean man pounds on our door making all kinds of threats and insults. He never goes away, or he might go away, but then he comes back again the next day. We basically end up living in fear and terror and are a prisoner of this problem. Here is how I handle problems like this.

When I see the mean man coming down my driveway, I grab my metaphoric baseball bat and I walk out my door, continuing all the way up to the gate of my fence line. As he approaches, I yell "What do you want!" as I am holding my metaphoric baseball bat, and possibly shaking with adrenaline. Before he even gets to my fence line, I order

141

him to stop. I ask him again what he wants. He tells me something about how I have screwed this up or that up or owe somebody money. I tell him I understand. He starts to approach. I order him to not come any closer and back off. I tell him I understand what he told me, and I will think about what he said and try to come up with a solution to take care of my obligations. I ask him if there is anything else. He says no. I say, "fine, have a good day." The mean man backs away, not sure what else he can say or do, because he is not sure if I am crazy, or how crazy I am. And that is EXACTLY what I want him to think.

You see the differences in the two examples above. In the first scenario, I tried to avoid the problem, hide, and coward from it. It was terrifying, I felt like a prisoner in my how home, and I solved nothing because the man is coming back. In the second scenario, I leaned into the problem. I anticipated it, saw it coming, and met it head on and did not let it inside my home territory. I did not let the man get to my door. I leaned into it and made sure I kept enough space for myself. I was a mouse barking like a huge nasty dog. I made it seem like I was not scared of him. I made him think twice about bothering me again. I also told him I would try to resolve the problem. So in that way I am going to try and actually solve the problem. But I will not be terrified or kept prisoner by this problem. I will control the environment, and I will deal with this problem on my own terms.

This is how you should be dealing with all problems. Anticipate, face it head on, and control it on your terms. Now for the rest of the process, we will use a similar procedure as we did for making decisions.

1. Clearly define the problem
2. Assemble all possible solutions
3. Create a pros and cons list for each solution
4. Test drive your solutions inside the Hunter Equation
5. Refine and adjust your solutions
6. Try to negotiate
7. Choose and execute your solution

Okay, so now you see why I needed to do a separate chapter for solving problems. Although the technical process is similar, the importance of facing the problem up front is more critical, and I added a couple new elements to the process. With that said, I am not going to copy/paste the same detailed description from the previous chapter. You can always refer back to the previous chapter if you want to read the detailed descriptions of each step again. However, I need to explain the new elements.

In step 1, obviously you need to clearly identify and define the problem. The first step in fixing a problem is admitting you have a problem. You do not even know you have a problem unless you can define it. So clearly define and understand what exactly your problem is in all of its details.

Step 2 is the most important and most difficult. As with making decisions in the previous chapter, this is your chance to seek outside advice. Do not be shy about doing this. A smart man thinks he knows all the answers. A wise man seeks out the advice of those who DO know the answers. So do not be afraid to ask for advice and help from those who might be able to offer it. At the same time, you need to take full ownership and responsibility of the problem. Don't dump it on someone else or expect someone else to solve it. The whole point of this book is for you to become fully empowered to handle and control all your own issues so that you do not depend on anyone else. Coming up with solutions to problems is a learning experience and an adventure unto itself. Embrace it. In fact, embrace the problem. Fully embrace it. Lean into it. Do you remember our chapter on eliminating fear, and how I talked about fully embracing and hugging the alligator? If you fully face, embrace, touch, and feel, it helps keep the fear down. Do not fear your problem. Eliminate your fear of the problem. Embrace it. Lean into it. Deal with it. You are warrior! Act like one.

Steps 3, 4, and 5 are the same as decision making. Make your pros and cons lists for each possible solution. Run your potential solutions inside the Hunter Equation to determine how External Factors and Random Luck might affect your outcome. Then refine and modify any of your solutions, while you eliminate the weakest possible solutions.

Now here's the thing. I've added step 6. Step 6 is to try and negotiate a better settlement of the problem. I have put the negotiation step toward the end on purpose. Most people would say, "Why don't you try to negotiate first?" The reason is that we need to fully understand and examine the problem, and our possible solutions, before we try to negotiate. This way, we fully understand what we are up against, how likely it is we have a good solution, and how horrible our solutions are. In other words, we know how desperate we are. If we have a great solution, then we can negotiate more aggressively. But if our solutions are horrible, then we know we need to be more flexible in our negotiations. Use your negotiation skills to try and reach a better settlement, solution, and outcome. You may or may not be successful. If you are successful, good for you. If you are not successful, then you will understand why I wanted you to have your possible solutions ready in case they are needed.

At this point, step 7 will be to take action on whichever solution you chose. You will either use a better solution due to your negotiation efforts, or you will use the best solution you produced during your problem-solving process. Either way, you will know you did the very best you could, and the solution you are instituting is the best possible solution at the time, given your circumstances and resources. That is all you control. You cannot control the entire world. Just focus on doing the best you can within the confines of what you control.

You might notice something about problem solving. You might notice that you may not always come up with a wonderful solution. It is what it is. The true nature of problem solving is not coming up with the perfect solution, because the perfect solution often does not exist. The true nature of problem solving is really more about FACING IT and not fearing it. It is about being proactive to solve it. Problem solving is not about being perfect. Problem solving is about not being afraid to play the game. Those who are a warrior and lean into battle with skill and strategy are the ones who Rise To Greatness.

Chapter Eighteen
Embrace Failure

The chapter title is not a typo. Some of you probably think I am crazy. Most of you by now should realize I am a little bit crazy. It actually helps to be a little bit crazy, but I digress. Embrace failure. Wow, sounds so horribly negative. If I were a Law of Attraction guru, I would be executed for saying that. Good thing I'm not. I am a realist. Okay, enough playing. Here is the deal. In order to succeed, you must embrace failure.

Most people who are successful have certain things in common. Successful people have usually failed at something in the past, or failed many times during their march to success. Successful people always keep trying, even after they fail. Successful people are not afraid to take risks. Successful people are not afraid of failure. In other words, successful people usually brush up against failure on and off and know it well, but never let failure stop them. So if you are going to be successful, you better get comfortable with failure and not let it scare you, bother you, or stop you.

In a way, this chapter is very similar to our chapter about eliminating fear, because here we are eliminating our fear of failure. We touched upon this subject in that chapter, but we have to give it more attention here. Failure is such a large issue and a main source of losing hope, that it deserves its own chapter. You will recall when we are going to eliminate a fear, we have to get close to it, stare at it, touch it, feel it, and wrestle with it. So here we go.

What is the definition of failure? My definition for our purposes is "Failure is an indication that your expected plan or goal was not reached as desired or expected." Is that fair enough? Were you expecting something grander? Were you expecting, failure is LOSER LOSER LOSER AWFUL SCARY HORRIBLE WORTHLESS CAN'T DO IT LOSER FAILED HOPELESS IMPOSSIBLE, ETC? Were you expecting the definition to look like the emperor from Star Wars with a beastly face and eyes and a black robe, and perhaps a sickle of death like the Grim Reaper? FAILURE is one of the most hated words. Just the sight of it evokes horrible feelings and traumas. I personally hate the word. But we all need to get over it. We need to get over the word and we need to get over ourselves in regard to our reaction to failure. It's just a word. It is just a word to indicate that our plan and goal was not reached as we desired or expected. It is a setback. Or delay. It is not the deathly end of the world, or declaration of our induction into the loser hall of fame. Let's stop giving the word so much power. That word does not own you. Failure does not own you. Failure is only an indication that your expected plan or goal was not reached as expected.

Failure is not a label. Failure is not the end. Failure is just a dashboard gauge that indicates your plan or goal was not reached yet. It means there will need to be some sort of modification to your plan or goal. Fine. So, modify your plan or goal. How hard is that? It's not a big deal. Nothing to be traumatized by, or fear.

Usually when a person is in the process of becoming successful, they will inevitably hit many setbacks and failures. The plan they had does not work, or they did not meet their goal as expected, or when expected. It happens all the time, and it's going to happen. EMBRACE this fact as an inevitability. Expect it, brace for it, and lean into it. Let's walk through a general scenario of the line of thinking a person needs to have when facing the expected failures and setbacks.

Perhaps you are starting a business. I know we have used this one before, but it's so common and relatable to most people, so forgive me. You have done your entire business plan, run everything through the Hunter Equation, and done everything else we talked about earlier. You are ready to execute your step-by-step plan, going from dot to dot, mini goal post to mini goal post.

Part of your thinking at this point needs to be "I'm possibly and likely going to have some setbacks and failures along the way." You are taking risks, although they are finely calculated risks. Whenever you try to do something difficult and complex, you are more than likely going to run into problems. It is reality. Some parts of your plan are going to fail. Does that scare you? It shouldn't. ACCEPT UP FRONT that parts of your plan are going to fail. EMBRACE this fact. You have already prepared some contingency plans in case certain External Forces or bad Luck hits you anyways. You know problems are coming. You just do not know when they are coming, or from which direction.

So, at this point, you know you will have problems, setbacks, and failures. You know some pieces of your plan will not be reached as expected or desired. Fact. You accepted this. But you don't fear it because you know it's coming. You know that when any piece of the plan fails, you will face up to it immediately and go through the process of problem solving that we covered previously. If you haven't noticed, you pretty much have all the skills you need at this point. We have gone over lots of things and your toolbox is full of goodies.

So, your adventure begins, and it's exciting and lots of hard work. You are not afraid of failures because you expect them, you know they will happen, and you know you will face them head on, and resolve them when they come. You also know every successful person has faced failure many times on their way to success. Plus, failure itself is only an indication you have to modify your plan or goal. No biggie.

Continuing with our scenario, we will say your first major failure occurs when you have a major setback, and something you were counting on working fails miserably and there is no way around it. Okay. You were expecting something like this to happen. It sucks that it happened, but it's no surprise. Deep breath. Use all your tools, my wonderful Jedi. No fear, examine the goal setting process you set up, examine your Hunter Equation carefully. Look at your Actions and External Forces specifically. Clearly identify what caused the failure. Do a complete post-mortem investigation. Find the flaws. Find the exact cause. Go into problem solving mode and find solutions to fix or go around the problem. Use the process, use your tools, use your intellect, and use your communication and negotiation skills if they can resolve this problem. Keep your emotions under control and do not panic. Believe in yourself and believe in your plan. Remember why you are fighting so hard to do what you are doing and reach your goal. All your tools need to come into play at once. This failure is only a test to see how well you use all your tools.

Pick yourself back up, figure it out, modify your plan or goal, and put in your new Actions and plan. Execute. Re-boot and start up again. It is a beautiful day because you are alive and living fully and you have skills to deal with this stuff now. You do not need to lose hope, mope around, and cry in the corner. Those days are behind you. Now you anticipate failures, accept them, embrace them, deal with them, and move on. That's how we roll.

Keep modifying your plan until you find something that works for you. Keep checking your Hunter Equation. Keep on your game. Do you notice there is no focus at all on FAILURE? The word and the event are not relevant anymore. The only thing that matters is how you deal with the situation, and how QUICKLY you deal with the situation. The faster you deal with it, the better off you will be. This is when you truly get enthusiastic about EMBRACING failure or leaning into it. A person can get to the point when a problem crops us and they think, "Oh good, let me immediately figure this out." It is an expected challenge actually. Step up to the challenge enthusiastically without fear or trepidation. My goodness, you are a true warrior Jedi now!

The other good thing about failure is that it gives you an amazing opportunity to learn important lessons. Struggling and resolving failures is how we learn and grow. Many of us have put together complex things like furniture, bicycles, gas grills, etc. Sometimes we screw it up and have to backtrack and take it apart again so we can fix the problem and put it back together again. I don't know about you, but when that has happened to me, I finish the project knowing WAY MORE than I ever wanted to know about the workings and construction of that item! But that is how we learn. Plumbers who screw up the job and have to fix what they have done, rarely make the same mistake again, and are far more knowledgeable and experienced after that. Business people who have failed later know all the things NOT TO DO, and that knowledge alone is worth its weight in gold. Failure is really the key to learning. This is why some parents actually let their kids do something stupid as long as they know they will not hurt themselves or someone else. A good parent knows that letting their kid fail in a controlled environment is the best education they could ever get. Failure = Learning + Growing. Oh wow, the makings of a new equation.

Are you starting to see why we embrace failure now? Just think how many of you thought the very notion was stupid or crazy at first. We embrace failure because we do not fear it, we fully expect it, we immediately deal with it, and we learn a tremendous amount from it. If you are going to Rise To Greatness, you need to see that failure is much smaller than you. You can handle it now. You are becoming amazing!

Chapter Nineteen
Quickly Adjust

One of the most important skills a person can acquire is the ability to quickly adjust to changing circumstances. There are numerous things a person may have to adjust to, such as changes in plans, circumstances, personal environment, financial changes, unexpected events, tragedies, traumas, losses, and so forth. You must be able to adjust to whatever situation is thrown your way or changes around you.

People who are unable to adjust to change usually become stuck and paralyzed easily. Change can throw you off your game very easily. If you are the type that has a fixed plan in your mind, and that plan always assumes all variables fixed, then you will for sure end up having problems. Obviously, when you are surrounded by many variables, one or more of them will change in a way you did not expect. If you are unable to adjust and adapt to the changes, you will be stopped in

your tracks and stymied as to what to do next.
work on this.

The entire premise of having to adjust is base
Change is another word people often do not like,
outright fear it. Change is something people like to p
exist, until it happens. I don't know about you, but th
sound similar to the last chapter about failure. Hmmm. S
we do with change? Embrace it perhaps?

Indeed. You will need to fully face change, accept it,
comfortable with it, touch it, feel it, and wrestle with it. Char.
reality of the Universe. One thing we know for sure is that thing
always changing. I have a phrase people hear from me all the t
where I say, "Nothing stays the same forever." People are alwa
annoyed when I say this because they THINK I am wrong and tha
there are many things that will and do stay the same. They are usually
thinking of their relationship, level of success, or how bad things are
for them. But of course, given enough time, many of these people find
themselves losing or changing their relationship, something happening
with their career (both good and bad), and basically everything they
thought was solid around them somehow changes eventually,
including horrible situations getting better. This is because change is a
constant of the Universe. How ironic. The one thing that never
changes is change. So we have to be brave, choose to wear our big
boy and big girl panties for the day, and fully accept and embrace that
most everything around you could change at any given moment.

Once you actually get over this huge mental mountain, things get
easier. After all, the worst part of change is the fact we never see it
coming, we never think it will come, and we live in total denial that it
will come. But it does. And it will.

By the way, the flip side of this is that if you are struggling and in
great pain right now, I can guarantee that it will change. The reason
why is because everything changes. People who are considering
suicide fail to realize that their life is DEFINITELY going to change
in the future. Nothing stays the same forever. So if you are struggling

.nk you cannot live this way forever, you need to realize that you
.ot need to live with way forever. Your life is guaranteed to
ge.

.Ve have not talked about it yet. It is not an issue for all of you.
: some of you are very depressed and have thought of suicide at one
.ne or another. I understand you. I have been there. I am not
,noring you, or the subject. This book is not about suicide or dealing
with depression, and I would not want to disrespect you or the issue
of suicide by writing a few paragraphs and claiming I covered it. I
cannot cover it in a few paragraphs, a chapter, or two chapters. It's a
separate book. But depression and suicide are important issues that
LOTS of people are dealing with. I know some of you are.

Again, I understand. I have been through many things, and
certainly know what depression and suicidal thoughts are like. I will
briefly say a couple things. First, your life WILL change. It is a
guaranteed fact. That is what this chapter is all about. Also, I can tell
you that depression fades over time. You won't feel like this forever,
even if change takes longer than you would like. Finally, you must
surely have some amazing things in your future if you stay around long
enough to receive them. I have seen it too many times over and over.
Eventually, you will receive relief from the pain, and you will be so
grateful you stuck around to enjoy your future. One more thing. You
have to consider the people around you. Try not to hurt those around
you. Also try to help those around you. It might be YOU who makes
a big difference in someone's life. If you were not around, you would
not be able to make that lasting contribution to that person and the
world.

I love you, and I want you to live. That is one reason I am writing
this book. Please accept what I offer here and continue with your
process of transformation, and then pay it forward by making the
world a better place, with you in it.

Back to change. So for various reasons above, we are deciding to
embrace change. We also anticipate change. We know it is going to
happen. So let us prepare for its arrival so that we can easily adjust.

In your Hunter Equation, you look at your possible External Forces. Change is part of that. Therefore, try to anticipate changes and make contingency plans for likely changes. This will allow you to adjust seamlessly and immediately. If you experience changes you never expected, simply go back to your Hunter Equation and review the equation, taking into consideration the changes you were hit with. The change will be entered into the External Factors element. Doing this will automatically require you to make changes to the Actions element. It might even change your Future Outcome element (your desired outcome/goal).

Change is not to be avoided. See it, face it head on, lean into it, deal with it. As quickly as possible, adjust your Hunter Equation, your plans, your step-by-step Actions, your goals, or make efforts to mitigate any damage. ADJUST.

Change can be opportunity. Remember our chapter on exploiting opportunity? Change is the perfect chance for you to use your skills in exploiting opportunity. Once the change happens, the dynamics of a situation will have changed. Some of it might be bad. But some of it may have hidden opportunities if you actually look for it instead of panicking and complaining about the bad parts. My advice is to be very quick about looking for opportunity during change, because usually the first person who sees it, gets it. When I was younger, I learned that I actually did really well in chaos. When things were stable, other people seemed to do better than I did because they had better contacts, more advantages, and they were efficient in a stable environment. BUT, if there was chaos and panic in the air, those people would seize up and fall over in a paralyzing fear due to such unfamiliar and uncertain events. I found that I could remain calm, sane, clear-minded, and if I acted very quickly, I could engage in some very good opportunities because all my competition was paralyzed in the chaos. I learned to love chaos and welcome it whenever it came. Change is the same thing. So embrace it.

I hope you have lost your dislike and fear of change. If it knocks you on the ground, get back up immediately. Review your equations and consider any new opportunities it has opened up. Mitigate any damage. Immediately put your new actions into motion. Have confidence in yourself, your abilities, and all the skills in your toolbox. Without thinking much about it, you will be quickly adjusting to any change or situation that comes your way.

Chapter Twenty
Know When To Hold'em & When To Fold'em

I was originally going to title this chapter "PERSISTENCE," but the more I thought about it, the more I realized it would be misleading, and even dangerously so. When most people think of "persistence," they think of "never stop" or "never give up." That can be a very good motto sometimes, but not always.

Persistence is a double-edged sword. On one hand, it is critical that you never give up at times when you become weak. But on the other hand, you have to know when to give up if something is never going to work. A person chiseling through a rock mountain to get to the other side would be a fool if he exercises too much persistence and never gives up. Obviously, it would be way smarter and more advantageous if he throws persistence out the window, gives up, and thinks of something else to do with his life. It is for this reason we have to examine both sides of persistence.

When I was younger, I considered persistence to be a way of life that you cling to, or you fail and die. I was that person who would chisel through a mountain my entire life, never give up, and never reach the other side. Persistence and discipline were never a problem for me. But as I became wiser, I realized that persistence is a tool rather than a way of life. Persistence is to be used when applicable and needed and set aside when intelligent logic dictates.

My first big lesson in this was when I started into sales while still going to school. I was enthusiastic and eager to be successful in sales, and I was willing to do anything, and do it until the end of time in order to reach the pinnacle of success. One problem. I was a horrible sales person. My personality at that time did not fit sales. I was kind of introverted, too honest and conservative in my presentations, and I would wait for people to come to me instead of me going to them, because I did not want to seem obnoxious or aggressive.

But the above facts did not discourage me from being persistent in my sales efforts for several years. The owner of the company I worked for became my mentor, and he actually tried to fire me twice, because as my mentor he knew sales was not going to work for me. But I was too persistent to even allow him to fire me. After being fired, I just kept showing up and kept trying. I was the poster child for persistence.

But finally, I had a mental shift and saw an opportunity to transition into something more administrative in nature. I tried it and was an immediate success. The administrative mind-set was a perfect fit for me. My life got better almost overnight when I FINALLY gave up the sales career. Thank goodness my persistence failed long enough for me to make that very necessary change in my life. If I had remained persistent and stayed in that sales job, I would still be there now and no better off. My biggest regret is that I did not give up on sales sooner. But unfortunately, I was just too persistent to give up.

On the other hand, I have had many instances in my life where persistence has been the key to my success. I have had times in my life where I just wanted to give up on what I was doing because I felt there was no hope of success. My innate persistence was the only thing that kept me going. Without my persistence, I would be nowhere now. In fact, I am not sure I would be alive now without persistence. I had days when I just wanted to give up on everything, including life. But I have this deep persistence that got me through to the next day. Where there is hope, there is persistence. I have also found that where there is persistence, there is hope.

Persistence has become my close friend. But my experience and wisdom has taught me when to sideline my persistence, and when to cling to my persistence for dear life. You must be able to do both, and you must be able to discern when to do each. Thus, this is what we need to explore.

Here is my general rule on persistence: *Always let persistence rule the day until you have factual logical proof that what you are doing will not work.*

I am letting that statement dangle up there alone because it stands on its own, is important, and you need to remember it. In the fog of war, you need to be able to recall that statement, and in a clear-thinking way determine your situation. In my example of being in sales, I should have concluded to set persistence aside because there was indeed factual logical proof that what I was doing would not work. The "factual logical proof" was the fact that my personality was the opposite of what was required for success in sales. Additionally, I had a long record of not succeeding in this sales job, despite my constant efforts. I should have seen this and given up sooner.

But there is a very important point I want to highlight. You will notice I say, "Always let persistence rule the day UNTIL you have factual proof..." This means that persistence gets the benefit of the doubt. If you are not sure there is factual logical proof, then you need to let persistence rule the day, and keep going with your mission. Without factual logical proof of eventual failure, you must stick with persistence and never give up. So, if you find yourself all tired and worn out saying, "Well I don't know if this will work or not," then that means you keep going and do not give up. You can only set persistence aside when you say, "I know this won't work because so on and so forth." It has to be an absolute statement of clear logical fact as to why your plan will fail before you give up.

The reason why is because if you are on a very difficult mission that will work with enough time and effort, you MUST remain persistent NO MATTER WHAT, or you will fail in that mission. If you believe in your mission and your plan, you must cling onto persistence as if it was your only lifeline. In Hunter Equation terms, I should have said, "If you believe in your Future Outcome and Actions, you must stick with persistence."

If at some point, you can clearly see factual logical proof that what you are doing will not work, then here is what you do. You stop and look at your Hunter Equation. Why have you determined that what you are doing won't work? You must be seeing a flaw in your Future Outcome (goal/mission), or you are seeing your Actions are flawed, or you are seeing an impending External Force that will surely destroy your plan, or possibly you see evidence of impending bad luck. Which is it exactly? So examine your equation and find the faulty piece. You may be able to modify part of your equation so that things can work again. What I am saying here is that having logical factual proof in itself may not be enough to totally abandon your goal. First, you must look at your equation to see if there is a way around the problem so that you can then continue with the goal and reinstitute your persistence. Only after determining that even the equation cannot be modified or repaired, should you totally give up on what you were doing.

But if you have determined it's a lost cause, please do stop. Do not waste your time and resources chiseling your way through a huge mountain. This is an example of when we call this adventure a failure and just move on. We do not care about failures. They don't scare us. Better to just embrace it, accept it, learn from it, adjust quickly, and move on immediately. Do not waste time. You can then come up with a new goal that excites you. The next goal and mission might be far better, and you will be glad the last one did not work out. This is how you look at life now right? I hope so.

With all that said above, let's assume that you have a mission you believe in, but it's going rough. You are tired, discouraged, and life is miserable. This is when you need to take persistence out of your toolbox and use it as a tool. Grab onto your persistence for dear life and never let go.

I have developed a few coping mechanisms I use when I am hanging on for dear life and cohabitating with my persistence. Firstly, remember everything you learned from the chapter on motivation. You need this now. So engage your motivational tricks. Primarily, remember why you are doing what you are doing. Remember that "happy place" of success I had you imagine when you were setting your goals. Bathe in that feeling of success at "Point B," as if you had accomplished your mission at the end-point. Doing this reminds you that the struggle is worth it. Using your motivational skills alongside your persistence is a valuable Jedi skill.

Another thing I do is "embrace the pain," the same as I embrace failure, and everything else I don't like. I just accept and embrace the pain of the struggle. Instead of being afraid of it or running away, I get used to it and comfortable with it. I accept that pain and discomfort is my neighbor for a while. Acceptance of things is usually a big part of any battle. Once you accept something instead of fearing it, sometimes it even just goes away.

Another trick I use is that I install small baby steps with small rewards. When you are struggling so hard that you feel as if you are crawling, your next mini goal post might seem too far away. So you need to break up the distance by creating more baby steps. Also, give yourself tiny rewards on a regular basis. If I am digging a hole and I just can't do it anymore, I would say to myself, "dig non-stop for 5 minutes, and then stop and drink your favorite beverage for 2 minutes." Then rinse and repeat. Someone watching you dig for short periods, then taking full beverage breaks, and so on, will think you are crazy. But we don't care what it looks like. Most of my successes in life have been very messy and scary looking. It's never pretty. I do not care how it looks. This is MY battle. I do what works for me. This is where you have to use everything I have taught you. You have to be your own person, do your own thing, and do what you know works for you to accomplish your mission.

You can see why this chapter is toward the end of the book. Using persistence requires intelligent disciplined discernment as to when to keep and hold it, and when to fold and bow out. Additionally, fueling your persistence in a very difficult tiring struggle requires all of the skills you have learned previously. This is real life now, and it's not easy. But if you apply yourself, you can do it. I hope you are seeing that now.

Chapter Twenty-One
Effective Leadership

Some of you might be wondering if a chapter on leadership is relevant to you. Perhaps you have no interest in being a leader, or a leadership role makes you feel uncomfortable. I am including this chapter because the fact is, once people see how self-empowered you are, they will likely assume you are suitable for a leadership role. People smell confidence, wisdom, and personal empowerment. You can just tell who has it, and who does not. Those that have it are naturally most suited for a leadership role within any group.

I am not suggesting that all of you now must become leaders. You don't have to if you don't want to, or if it does not fit your personality. But what I am saying is that you should not be surprised if others look up to you more as a leader now than they did before. Even with just a strong sense of self, you will have the energy of someone who is strong with leadership qualities. Thus, I am including this chapter to briefly discuss the issue for those who need it, and those who might end up needing it at some point.

Being a leader does not mean you are the smartest, strongest, loudest, or the best. That is not what being a leader is about. In fact, the BEST sales person in a company should not be the leader. The best sales person in the company should be the best sales person in the company making as many sales as possible. The smartest person in the company should be the person solving all the problems and anticipating what is coming, such as a chief operating officer. The strongest person in the company should be the top support person who keeps all the key people moving, going, and productive. The loudest person in the company might be the cheerleader or disciplinarian. So who is the leader? Ahhhh, I'm so glad you asked. The leader should be the best communicator and motivator.

The job of a leader is to keep everyone motivated and working together in harmony so that the company can reach its goals. It's that simple. A leader is responsible for the company reaching its goals. Whether you work for yourself, or you answer to a higher boss or board of directors, you as the leader are responsible for the group reaching its set goals.

How will you reach the goals? That is your job after all. Therefore, that should be your focus. To accomplish this, will you make all the sales, or do all the tasks yourself? Impossible. So do not try. A true leader recognizes the true talents of all the people working WITH them. I would say "under them," but you are about to see that is not my leadership style.

A leader organizes all the right people to do all the right tasks, and then plays a supporting role in seeing they perform to the highest of their potential.

That is what a leader is. As a leader, you would first develop a "sense of self" profile for each person on your team. This means you need to do for the team member what you did for yourself. It means taking inventory of all their skills, abilities, strengths, weakness, and so on. You need to clearly understand and know each person on your team. This is the only way you can know which person should be doing which task.

Then as the leader, you determine the group's goal and develop the plan to achieve the goal. Basically, just do for the team what you have done for yourself. Clearly define your goal, do your Point A to Point B, set up your mini goal posts in between, and so forth. Get out the Hunter Equation to assist in the construction and testing of your plans.

At this point you have a full understanding of each team member, and you have a full understanding of your team's goal and game plan. Now you just need to get your team to interact with your plan. This is when you step up as a master communicator. You must very effectively communicate the team's goal and plan to each team member so that all team members clearly understand. The chapter we did on being a master communicator is very important and you need to follow all the details, such as speaking in their language, and getting them to engage with what you are saying at their level. You are not speaking AT anyone. You are speaking WITH everyone, but on their terms of engagement so that you get better results from them.

You will then engage your motivational skills to motivate your team to reach their goal. You will negotiate through any difficulties and conflicts. You will enforce discipline and persistence, so the group completes their mission without going astray. Don't you see it yet? YOU have ALL the skills necessary to be the leader. You ARE the leader. Only someone with all of these skills is qualified to be the leader.

I got a little ahead of myself to make the point about how you already have leadership skills. Now I want to put the focus back on a leader's most important contribution, which is being a communicator. Remember, your job is to be the best communicator. You are the grease that keeps all the wheels and parts moving, and the fuel that keeps the engine running. The grease makes sure all the separate moving parts work together in harmony. The fuel for the engine keeps the entire team running toward the common goal. So you are the grease and the fuel. You are the communicator and the motivator.

You work for them! You read that right. As the leader, you work for them. The grease is the support system for the moving parts. The grease does not actually do the work. The grease just allows the moving parts to do the work. The grease must make sure the parts are moving. The job of the grease is to make the part's life more efficient and effective, thus the grease works for the part. The fuel to keep the engine running is the same thing. The fuel does not do the work. The engine does the work. The fuel just gives the engine what it needs to do all the work. So as the fuel, your job is to give the engine what it needs to do all the work. Therefore, you work for the engine.

The above analogy translates fairly literally in real life. If I were the leader of a team, I would have all the correct team members working on all the correct tasks that match their skill-sets. But then I need to be the grease. This means I will go to each team member and see if they have all the resources, they need in order to do their jobs. I would literally say to each team member, "Is there anything I can get you?" "Is there any way I can help you do your job more effectively?" I would literally act as if I work for them. Because I do. As the grease, I must make sure the moving parts have everything they need.

My other job as the grease is to be sure each moving part is working well with the other moving parts. So my job will be to make sure there is clear effective communication between each team member. Not all team members are master communicators. They did not read this book yet. So some of the team members will be frustrated about relating to others effectively. They might not know how to effectively communicate conflicts they are having with each other. It is your job to be the master communicator and communicate FOR the team members that are unable to do it effectively. As the grease, you must make sure all moving parts work smoothly together.

So again, in real life, you would ask each team member if everything is going okay on their end. If a team member expresses a concern about how the moving parts are cooperating, it is your job to then effectively communicate the issues between all team members. You are a moderator of sorts. This is why you hopefully paid close attention to that communication chapter. You will also end up applying negotiation skills in doing all of this.

Some leaders think it is there job to say, "Shut up and do your job," "Mind your own business," or "If you can't do your job, leave." That is not effective leadership. With effective leadership, you work for the team. So, it is your obligation to figure out how you can get each person to work effectively at their full potential. Your job is to smooth communications and conflicts between the team. You have a full-time job as the master communicator.

Your other job is to be the fuel for the engine. You must be sure all team members have all the resources required to do their job. Fuel is required for the engine to run. Your job is to make sure the engine has fuel and never stops running. In my personal opinion, the leader would be responsible for running to the store and buying more pencils if the team were about to run out of pencils and their work would stop. If pencils are a form of fuel, it would be your job to make sure they don't run out. Hopefully, you have a team member in charge of acquiring resources the team needs, but still the same, YOU are ultimately in charge of making sure all resources are on hand without interruption.

Being the fuel in keeping the engine running also means you are the chief motivator. Pull out all your motivational skills and apply them here. You will also need your negotiation skills, because you are essentially trying to get something you need from another person. That was part of our definition of negotiation. You are negotiating with a team member to get them to provide their work and expertise, so that your team will reach its goal.

So how will this negotiation factor work in this scenario? Same as in the negotiation chapter. You will first LISTEN to each team member while you are doing your original assessment of their skills and abilities. You will listen for what they truly want and need, right? Yes, it may be money. But you might see some other things also. Some team members might respond really well to special attention. Some might respond well if they have an extra half hour added to their lunch break because they have to drive across town back home and walk their dog. You, having the consideration for that special need they have, might make all the difference in the world to that team member, and earn you their undying loyalty. Whatever it is, you need to figure out what they truly want and need. Then strive to provide it. Again, you work for them. So, you are trying to give them what they want and need so that they will function at their highest potential within your engine.

Your job is to encourage your team. Use all your motivational skills; but remember that one size does not fit all. You will need to handle each team member slightly differently. This special unique treatment and relationship with each one will also earn you more devotion and loyalty from them, because they will see you care enough to give them unique special attention. I know it sounds like a lot of work, but it's your job! You work for them! So do whatever is necessary to keep that engine running smoothly. If you do your job and the engine runs well, your team will inevitably reach its goal. If the team reaches its goal, that makes you a hero. The higher-up bosses will give you all the credit. You can laugh to yourself knowing that you were basically just talking to co-workers and running to the store for pencils.

One important thing to remember is that you lead by example. All the team members will be always watching. Therefore, you need to act in accordance with how you want your team members to act. If you want your team members to act in a positive kind way, you need to act in a positive kind way. If you want your team members to show up early, then you need to show up early. If you want your team members to care about quality, then you need to care about quality. If you want your team members to listen, then you need to always listen. You get the idea. Leading by example is actually a very effective tool for shaping how your team behaves. It is very non-verbal. Just by behaving a certain way, you can affect how they behave. You are the leader after all.

This entire chapter was pretty much one giant analogy involving a work situation. But I don't want it lost upon you that effective leadership can also be used within your home life. Perhaps consider your family members, such as your kids, as team members. You can get the household operating more smoothly if you use these leadership techniques at home.

Being an effective leader is not just about working in a career. Being an effective leader can be used in every-day life. Most people out there are pretty lost and wander aimlessly whenever something needs to be done. Imagine having no knowledge of anything in this book. A person would just be stumbling around in the dark. Having these skills and living as if you are a leader is very empowering and smart. It is a great way to carry yourself and present yourself. People will think you have risen to greatness.

Chapter Twenty-Two
Evaluate Your Relationships

Once you have spent so much time and effort reconstructing yourself, it only makes sense that you will need to take a close look at all your relationships by evaluating and reevaluating them, to see how the new you fits into them. There are two main reasons for doing this.

The first reason is very similar to how people in recovery from addictions need to change their relationships. There are some people that will be toxic to your new way of being. They may have issues with the new person you have become. If there were people in your life who were able to manipulate you, control you, abuse you, use you, or toy with you, they will have a difficult time doing that since you have made your personal transformation to a greater person. They will reject the new you and try to tear you back down to the old person you were, so that they can continue using you and treating you as they had been. Obviously, you cannot allow this to happen.

You have hopefully come very far on your journey and are a different person now. But this is new for you and you are still very fragile. Believe me when I tell you that one toxic negative powerful person in your life can tear you back down to nothing in about five minutes if they push the right buttons. EXPECT THIS. Brace for it. Be ready to exit the situation and conversation quickly and let it roll off of you. With that said, you are possibly going to have to reevaluate your relationship and amount of contact with this person if you want to continue progressing in your transformation process. This is exactly the same as how a recovering addict cannot hang out with his substance abusing friends once he is recovering and sober. Some people are just not good for you to be around anymore, even if you enjoyed them in the past.

The second reason is that you have changed. You are not the same person anymore. For this reason, you need to see if you are still compatible with certain people. Prior to your transformation, maybe doing nothing and living day to day was good enough for you, and that is what worked for your current relationship. But after your transformation, you might have other goals and interests. Maybe you want to get healthy and live healthy. Maybe you want to join some activity clubs. Maybe you want to travel. Maybe you want to try new hobbies or a new career. Obviously being stuck in a relationship with someone who has been content to do nothing will not work for you anymore.

Additionally, you will want to look at your interactions with those around you. You have changed, and you have changed your approach of how you deal with people. You may need to change and re-build your relationship with people that you did not treat very well before. You may have fences to mend and relationships to repair. The dynamics in your relationships will have changed, so you will need to reflect those changes in how you interact with others.

For all the reasons above, I feel it is important for you to examine all your relationships. I do not want any of your relationships to derail you and ruin your good work. I also want you to recognize that you may need to pay some attention to relationships that deserve repair.

YOUR RELATIONSHIP WITH YOURSELF

I hope you have learned that your relationship with yourself is the most important relationship you will ever have. It needs to come first above all others. If you don't have a good relationship with yourself, you won't have a good relationship with anyone else.

You have seen from the beginning of this book that personal transformation starts from within. We have spent the better part of this book on self-examination, coming to peace with yourself, getting to know yourself, and getting to love yourself. Your relationship with yourself is what this book is all about. Please tell me you get that now.

Thus, this is a good time to do a self-check and evaluate how you are doing with your relationship with yourself. Do you like yourself? Are you comfortable with yourself? Do you know yourself? How are things going with yourself?

By now you realize that if you have any negative responses to the above, I am just going to send you back to Chapter 2 right? You know this, right? Yes, I think you do. I also have told you that it is totally okay if you need to go back and revisit prior chapters. In fact, it would be abnormal for a person to easily do a transformation without any kind of setback, revisit, or review. Setbacks are inevitable, and there might be times you need to refresh your memory on certain things or regain confidence in other things.

So this is a chance for you to evaluate your relationship with yourself. Check yourself. Do it often. If you have a problem, or have doubts, go back and have a talk with yourself. Figure out if some piece of junk needs to be removed, or if you need to clear out some fear or old frustration. Remaining healthy and happy requires maintenance, so expect to do maintenance on the relationship with yourself.

YOUR RELATIONSHIP WITH MARRIED PARTNER

I have purposely isolated out marriage because it has additional legal and financial complications that other romantic relationships do not have. This is all the more reason why it's critical you evaluate your relationship with your married partner. You are in your process of transformation. You are changing and are a different a person now.

Based upon this premise, how do you feel about your marriage now? There are two possible answers here.

You might feel better about your marriage. Perhaps your marriage was great before, and now it can be even greater. Or perhaps your marriage had problems before, but now you feel the new person you have become can make this marriage a success. You are happier within yourself, so that makes it possible for you to love someone else more effectively. You also are a better communicator, and marriage is all about communication. You also more clearly see all of your own shortcomings that may have hurt the marriage, and you are in a position to fix those or avoid them now. Whatever the case may be, take a close look at how you can improve your marriage now that you are the new you.

On the other hand, you may have determined now more than ever before that this marriage is simply not working for you. Perhaps it was the marriage itself that was toxic, and dragging you down, and keeping you down. You would see that clearly now more than before.

If you have determined that your marriage is toxic and going nowhere, you really have to face the reality on that. You would then have two choices. Stay in the toxic marriage for whatever your reasons, and limit your growth in this transformation process, OR you would have to make a major change and transition out of this marriage so that you can be free to fully transform into the person and into the life you want. Neither is easy. Life isn't easy. But do not be afraid. Go back to the chapter on eliminating fear. You will need to eliminate fear on this one. Use the Hunter Equation to do an analysis of your various choices with this relationship. Ask yourself if you are free to be you in this relationship. Ask yourself how you will end up years from now if you stay, or if you go. Use everything I have taught you to analyze the situation. I cannot tell you what to do because your situation is complicated, and you are the one that has to live with the consequences, not me. But I have faith you are better equipped to evaluate this situation than you were before.

RELATIONSHIP WITH SIGNIFICANT OTHER

We have talked about your marriage. If you are not married, but are in an established relationship, engaged, cohabitating, or just dating, this section is for you. As with a marriage above, you need to evaluate how you feel about the relationship and how it is going. I do not need to repeat everything I said above. The reason your relationship with a "significant other" is different, is because the bar for making a change is much lower. You are not legally bound to this person. Certainly, if you are just dating them and living separately, you are even less bound.

So my advice to you is more strict. If your current relationship does not fit like a glove in your new life as your new person, then the relationship is probably not for you. The old you would have accepted much lower standards so that you would not be alone. But now you should not have any huge hang-ups about being alone. You are not afraid to be alone, and you enjoy being with yourself, so being alone should not be as much of an issue for you as it was before. Plus, who says you will be alone for long? You might meet the perfect new person next week.

Remember, now that you are a much greater person, you are also much more appealing to other people. Other people will see and sense that you have a greater sense of self-empowerment and power in general. It makes you more appealing and intriguing. Very likely, a higher caliber of person will now have interest in you. If you keep yourself stuck in your old dead relationship that no longer fits, you will miss out on meeting that higher caliber person that is a much better fit for you.

Your relationship going forward should reflect who you are as a person and where your life is going. The relationship needs to be compatible with the new you, your new life, and the direction in which your life is heading. If it is toxic or does not fit, it is not for you. There is something better out there for you. Stop limiting yourself. Those days are over. The new you no longer limits or blocks your own progress and dreams.

Obviously, same as with the marriage in the section above, if you are happy with your current relationship, then by all means continue and make it better. Certainly, you are much better equipped now to improve your relationship and make it better for both you and your partner.

YOUR RELATIONSHIP WITH YOUR KIDS

If you have kids, you need to evaluate your relationship with them. You have learned new skills about communication, negotiation, and living with love. Those three chapters alone are invaluable in dealing with your kids. The entire book will help you with your kids. But just looking at those three chapters I mentioned, you might change how you deal with your kids.

It is important for all people involved, that you have a loving, supportive, positive, and responsible relationship with your kids. Your kids need strong guidance and limits, but also need love 100% of the time, and support even when they are taking a wrong turn. I realize those who have kids have their hands full, and anything I say is just talk, and walking the walk is way harder. But please consider my concepts in dealing with them.

I have done a lot of work with young people. I know the weak-points. They are:

1. Lack of involvement, guidance, limits, discipline from parents
2. Lack of love and attention from parents
3. Parents are too strict, too much discipline with older teens
4. Lack of support when a teen struggles.

Please consider if you are guilty of any of the traps above. If you just remember two things about your relationship with your kids, it is to give them constant unconditional love, even if they are making mistakes and screwing up; and secondly to COMMUNICATE. If you show your kids love and communicate constantly, you will see an improvement in your relationship with them without even doing anything else.

This is not a book on raising kids. I am not saying I know everything about raising kids. But I would be remiss if I did not include the importance of your relationship with them in this book. Evaluating your relationship with your kids, and making beneficial changes to improve that relationship, is reason enough to write this book and to have you read this book.

YOUR RELATIONSHIP WITH YOUR FAMILY

What I mean by your relationship with your family is your parents, siblings, and relatives etc. Many of us have dysfunctional relationships with one or more of our family members. We are kind of stuck with our family, so divorcing them or never seeing them again is not usually an option.

But what I suggest is that you examine each family relationship you have. For some, you may decide to limit contact. For others, you may decide to increase contact. For others, you may decide there are things you can do to fix or improve the relationship. You need to act accordingly. My hope is that your personal transformation not only improves yourself personally, but also improves all your relationships and your family dynamics.

YOUR RELATIONSHIP WITH YOUR FRIENDS

Your relationship with your friends has an even lower bar for making changes, than any of your family or romantic relationships. Basically, if you have friends who are toxic, hold you back, drag you down, or simply don't fit into your new life, you probably need to gently, silently, and politely, detach. It's that simple. You cannot have periphery people destroying the life you are trying to build here. I suppose I could continue on, and talk about your boss, co-workers, mail delivery person, dog-walker, and so forth, but I feel you have the flavor for what I am talking about. The point is that you have come too far into the transformation process, and I first and foremost want to make sure none of your relationships destroy your state of mind that you have been building. You must protect the new you, because that is the dream and the Promised Land you have been building and trying to reach. We are in essence building a dream of freedom, hope, and excitement for yourself. We don't need a couple of toxic people tearing you down and causing you to give up, and having you end up back in that old house and debris pile in which we first found you. Please do not let it happen. I have too much hope for you.

Chapter Twenty-Three
Finding Your Passion

Most of this book has been about clearing out baggage, finding yourself, figuring out who you are, getting to know yourself, and developing all the skills you need to reach your full potential. We have looked at what is behind you, and all around you. We have looked at goal setting as a way to look forward. But our discussion is not complete until we talk about finding your true passion so that you are fully looking forward in the correct direction.

In order for a person to have a strong drive and motivation, they need a passion. So yes, I could have covered this in the motivation chapter, but I wanted to wait until you had a full toolbox of skills, knowledge, and self-awareness before talking about finding your passion. The reason is, that finding your passion requires you to have no fear, no limits, and absolute confidence that you are worthy of any pursuit.

I have not mentioned the word "self-esteem" often, but the entire book is about building your self-esteem. A high self-esteem allows you the freedom and confidence to ALLOW YOURSELF to pursue your true passion in life. Comments and judgments from others will not stop you from being who you truly are inside, and from pursuing your passion.

Thus, I now feel it is time for us to discuss pursuing your passion and achieving greatness in whatever you choose. That was another point of the book. But what if you are not sure what your passion is?

Do not be discouraged or feel awkward if you are unsure of your passion. A surprising number of people have trouble identifying their passions in life. It all starts in high school when many students have absolutely no clue what they want to do with their lives. This struggle often continues in college, and results in changing majors or dropping out altogether. So, you are not alone by a long shot if you still have not figured out your life passions.

Finding your true passions is sort of like finding yourself. Or should I say it is sort of like finding your Sense Of Self. Therefore, we might consider going through the same process as we did for developing your sense of self. Lots of questions, and lots of lists.

What inspires you? What sort of thing when you see it makes your ears perk up? Well, if you could answer that, maybe you would already know your passion, right? But use a question like this to give you clues. For example, do you feel inspired and elevated when you are around kids? Or animals? Or helping people? Or nature? If any of those give you a sense of elevation, happiness, or inspiration, then it is likely your passion is RELATED to that subject matter.

That does not mean that if you are inspired by kids you should become a teacher. You might say to me that being a teacher is the scariest thing you ever heard of and not for you. But perhaps something else involving kids is your passion. You have to use your imagination. For example, helping to coach a youth sport, or working at an Aquarium giving tours to kids, or becoming a youth counselor, etc. There are many things related to working with kids that do not involve walking into the belly of the beast, such as being a teacher.

If you are inspired by nature, what does that mean? Well, it means possibly working at a national or state park. It means working in forestry. It might even mean doing odd jobs clearing forest or landscape areas for private homeowners. Maybe it means offering your services as a gardener in your neighborhood. Or maybe it means going into law enforcement as a Game Warden. You see, there are many hard-core or gentle ways to engage in whatever your passion is.

So the first question to ask yourself is what types of vocations, people, animals, places, or things, inspire you. I knew a guy once who LOVED cars and got a job installing high-end brakes for a specialty brake company. Some might have called him a mechanic or a blue-collar worker, but this guy was living his passion and loved his job. Someone else might choose to go into car sales. The possibilities are endless.

It is really up to you to ask yourself the question of what inspires you. Then do not be afraid to explore different possibilities within your answer. The inner thought of "that is not realistic" is not acceptable. Anything is realistic if you can create a workable equation to achieve it. Just stick in your desired result into the Future Outcome and fill out the rest of your equation until it makes sense and is doable.

My next favorite question to ask is "What do you love doing?" This is different from what inspires you. What inspires you has to do with what perks up your interest and your spirit. What you love doing is all about your existing likes and interests. So, what do you love doing?

Do you like reading? Do you like exercising? Do you like computers? Do you like socializing? What are your hobbies you enjoy doing? If you have free time or go on vacation, what do you enjoy doing most with that free time? These questions will result in answers involving things you currently love doing.

With the list of activities, you love doing, consider all relevant occupations involving them. If you love exercise, consider working at a gym or going into personal fitness coaching. If you love flying toy airplanes, consider taking a class that is aviation related, and might get your foot in the door into some aviation job. If you like socializing, consider being a host or hostess, or going into sales. If you like traveling, consider being a flight attendant (tough job though, yikes). Or consider being a traveling sales person.

You really need to open your mind and consider all the possible permutations of involving things you love to do. Do not limit yourself. Taking a class or multiple classes to do something you have a passion for is totally within the realm of reality. There are very often financial aid and educational loans available. There are local colleges and online courses. No excuses anymore. Plus, if it is your passion, it is likely you will actually enjoy the educational experience required.

So write down everything you love doing, and then write a list of all possible occupations associated with those things. Nothing is off limits at this point.

Another question I like to ask is, "In a perfect world, what would you see yourself doing in five years?" Assuming your answer is not "nothing," or "drinking on a beach," the answer could give a clue as to what direction to look. For example, if your answer is that you see yourself in a warm climate working part time to help people, this might be illuminating in more ways than one. This might be showing you that your true passion is to live in a different location. Perhaps you need to look at transitioning to a more desirable location. Just plug that location into your Future Outcome and fill out the rest of the equation to see what Actions might be required to make that happen.

Then, you can consider what occupations might be available, taking into consideration that new location. Plus, you can explore what you feel you meant by "help people" part time. Using your fantasies and imagination can give you the ideas and clues, as to what your heart and soul really yearns for.

Finding your passion is all about communicating with your heart and soul. What feeds your soul? What makes you feel complete? What would make you feel complete? What is food for your soul? Finding your passion is achieved by your ability to effectively communicate with your inner self.

If you ask yourself enough questions, and listen carefully to the answers, you will find clues and ideas to explore. This is a self-exploration exercise in reality. As I mentioned, we could have very well included this at the beginning of the book when we talked about our sense of self. But if I had talked about it then, you would have put all kinds of limits on yourself. We are talking about it now because you hopefully have a new outlook, and you certainly have many more life skills at your disposal than before.

But the process of self-examination and looking into yourself is how you find such answers. I will give you another hint that will also become a recurring theme for you. Where you feel love is likely a clue toward your passion. Love inspires. So where the love is, you will find inspiration. Where you find inspiration, you will find your passion. Part of your reward for your Rise To Greatness is for you to experience and enjoy your true passions.

Chapter Twenty-Four
Learning & Growing

An essential part of greatness for any person is for them to always and consistently be on a path of learning and growth. I don't care how old you are, how experienced, or how smart you are. This rule applies to everyone. Remaining on a path of personal growth is what keeps you alive and healthy. Your momentum of energy must always be moving in a forward direction. If at any time, you remain stagnant or reverse in direction, you will begin to suffer decay, pain, and increased failure. Therefore, no matter what you do, take at least small steps forward every day toward learning and growth.

This book is only one moment of your long journey. I obviously hope you have been gaining plenty from it, but please realize that you will need to continue your transformation beyond this book. You are a growing, amazing person. You do not need to learn only one small finite set of items and live with them. You should be learning infinitely and growing infinitely. If you read *The Hunter Equation* book, you know that I talk about how this one life is just a small part of the huge journey our eternal soul is taking. Our eternal soul is on a mission to learn and evolve with each lifetime. Let this lifetime be a valuable and significant one. Let us now explore some of the different areas of growth.

CONSTANT SELF-CHECKING

It is important you are always running maintenance on yourself. You have done much work to become more in-tune with yourself. This requires maintenance so that you remain in-tune with your inner self you worked so hard to discover and build.

This means constantly running tests, which is my way of saying to constantly ask yourself questions. You might ask, "Am I happy?" "Why not?" "Do I feel afraid of anything?" "What is bothering me?" "Do I love myself?" "What is my opinion of myself?", and "Why do I feel that way?" Questions, questions, questions. Pretend you are a parent trying to talk to your teenager. Ask yourself lots of probing questions in an effort to stimulate thought within yourself and start a self- examination. Basically, what I am suggesting you do, is go back to the chapter on sense of self and re-examine your current status.

Examining and building your sense of self once is not enough to remain healthy and vibrant indefinitely. You must go back and make sure everything is the way it should be, and you still feel you are constructed how you wish to be constructed. People very often perform renovations on their home and love them, but then years later totally renovate again. You might find in some time that you want to go through this book again and renovate again. Another example is how perfectly working airplane engines are taken apart on set schedules to be sure none of the parts have unseen defects. Preventative maintenance can save time, money, and lives. This applies for you as well.

STRENGTHS, WEAKNESSES & INVENTORY

While you are in the chapter about building your sense of self, performing maintenance, don't forget to also review your lists of strengths and weaknesses. Also review your inventory of skills and abilities. This is all part of remaining in close communication and in-tune with yourself.

Re-doing your lists of strengths and weaknesses on and off is a great way to evaluate any progress you have made on eliminating weaknesses and building strengths. You may need to remove some weaknesses on the list and add some strengths to the list. You also may become inspired to begin extra work on certain weaknesses or strengths.

You will also recall that as part of exploiting opportunities, you must be fully current and informed of all your available abilities, skills, and resources. Therefore, reviewing this is required so that you are fully in touch with everything you currently have to offer if opportunities arise.

Periodically doing a full review of yourself can really give you perspective on how far you have come, or what you still need to work on. But the most important purpose is to ensure that you remain very closely connected with knowing who and what you really are. That was kind of the point of the whole book, wasn't it? Therefore, I do not want all your good work to go to waste by having all this fade away with time. Thus, revisit all this often to keep it fresh.

RE-EVALUTE YOUR GOALS

Like everything else I mentioned previously, it is beneficial to review your goals periodically. What I really should be saying is review your Hunter Equation periodically.

Review your Future Outcome (goal/desired outcome) and be sure it is still in alignment with who you are, and what you truly desire. Goals can change with time, and there is nothing wrong with that. The only thing to make it wrong would be if you lose track of who you are and where you want to go. Therefore, frequent review of your goals is very beneficial to making sure you are still on track for what you really want and believe in.

While you are looking at your goals, review the rest of your Hunter Equation. Are your planned Actions still relevant and complete? Are there any additional External Forces you should be anticipating? Are there any additional factors of luck you are vulnerable to, or that might even be in your favor? Review the entire equation to be sure it is still sound, accurate, and in alignment with your true feelings and mission (which is your Intent). The entire equation needs to balance and work together for a good outcome.

ALWAYS REFINING AND IMPROVING

While you are examining yourself, your capabilities, goals, and your equation, be sure to take this opportunity to initiate any modifications, refinements, or improvements to any of the above.

Usually when we do periodic reviews of operations, we notice ways we can improve the operation. We may not have noticed these opportunities for improvement before because we did not have the knowledge and experience that we have now. As you become wiser and more experienced, you will notice things now that you did not notice before. Therefore, it is often fruitful to look at your operations and yourself from time to time so that you can see things you did not see before. You can use this opportunity as a time for self-improvement.

INCREASE YOUR KNOWLEDGE BASE

Constantly gaining knowledge is a great way to keep your mind engaged and evolving. Please take any opportunity to learn something new every day. Enrolling yourself in a community class is a great way to learn something new and socialize with new people. Reading books is another great way to gain an expanse of knowledge on different subjects.

But the most effective way to gain knowledge is by engaging with a mentor and enjoying the experience of doing things. Do not be afraid to try new things that you have never done before. Learning to do new things only expands your breadth and depth as a person. You will not become a master at everything you try. That is not the point. The point is to have the experience of engaging with so many different genres of skills, subjects, and thoughts. A vast expanse of knowledge and experience is one of the most valued assets a person can have.

EMOTIONAL EVOLUTION

Continuing to master your emotions is a life-long task and journey. Nobody does this in one book, one day, one month, or one year. Mastering your emotions is something we can get a handle on, but it is not something where our work is ever completely done.

Be mindful of always working to improve your emotional health. Be asking all those questions about how you feel and how you are doing emotionally. Be prepared to sometimes receive answers you did not want to hear. The negative feedback from your own mind will tell you what you should be focusing on for improvement.

Your emotional well-being is critical to your success and happiness as a person. You must constantly run self-checks to determine if you have any problems that need immediate attention. I have stressed in this book about confronting, facing up to, and leaning into any issues that need attention. That is especially true with your emotional health and state of mind. Without a strong emotional well-being, you will have trouble operating at full capacity up to your full potential. You will have trouble reaching your goals. This would be equivalent to letting your car run out of oil. That one little thing can destroy the whole thing. Check your oil often and never run out. Are you sick of my analogies yet? Yes, I realize I should seek professional help. But I will use whatever tools necessary to help you understand and reach your new level of greatness.

SPIRITUAL GROWTH

In this book I am not discussing religion, spirituality, or lack of either. This book is for your own personal growth and development regardless of what religious or spiritual views you may hold.

However, I would be remiss if I did not mention your spiritual growth as being important. Whatever type of faith or spirituality you engage in, be sure it is in alignment with your true beliefs and morality. That in itself is a self-check moment.

But more than that, use your spiritual connections to gain comfort and inspiration for your life. If it works for you, then use it as a tool to drive your growth and desire to be a better person. Anything in your toolbox that helps you achieve and maintain your greatness is an advantage worth having.

A FINAL REMINDER

Just a final reminder of how important learning and growing is. Keeping yourself engaged in a constant process of growth is essential to keeping hope alive. Hope is life. Where there is self-improvement, there is hope that you can do better and achieve more. Therefore, as long as you are learning and growing, you can be rest assured that you are creating a more hopeful tomorrow.

Chapter Twenty-Five
Rise To Greatness

We have come so far together. All of you started in different circumstances when we started this journey. Some of you were already doing well and wanted to do even better. Some of you were really struggling. Some of you were in pain. Some of you felt hopeless. All of you had one thing in common. You all wanted more for yourselves and your lives.

In the beginning of this book, I offered my hand to you. I offered to help you up. All I could do was offer my hand and the advice contained in this book. You were the one who had to decide if you loved yourself enough to try for better. You had to be the one to put forth the effort to learn and be better. You were the one who had to decide to change. I could not make you want to be better. I could not make you strive for improvement. I could not make you read this book. My contribution was small. I dedicated this book to you. You are the true hero. You are the true inspiration. You dared to become greater than you were.

I have tried my very best to teach you everything I could. I apologize to you for anything I may have missed, fallen short on, or left out. You all are deserving of the very best. I do not pretend to be perfect, or the holder of all knowledge on Earth. None of us are perfect. What matters is that we try to be the best people we can be. The best we can be to each other, and the best we can be to ourselves.

I do ask something of you. Please use everything you have learned to love yourself more, and love others more. The world needs more love. All of us reading this have experienced hurt and pain that we do not wish to ever repeat, nor would we wish it upon others. What was lacking in some of our lives was love and encouragement when we needed it most. I ask that you pay it forward and reach out to someone, or others, who need love and encouragement right now.

One question I have not answered in this book is likely the biggest question you have. How can I be happy? You might ask why I didn't have an entire chapter devoted to that. After all, you would be willing to read an entire book if it just answered that one question, right?

The reason I did not have a chapter on finding happiness is because each of you must find your happiness in your own way. But there is an even more involved and accurate answer. The truth is that happiness is not a destination. Happiness is a journey.

But happiness is even more than that. Happiness is knowing that you found yourself. Happiness is being comfortable with yourself. Happiness is loving yourself. Happiness is the fulfillment and satisfaction of facing adversity and overcoming it. Happiness is achieving a desired personal transformation. In other words, happiness comes from within. I cannot give you happiness. Nobody can. You are the only person who can give yourself happiness.

You can give yourself happiness by self-realization, self-worth, self-validation, accomplishment, self-improvement and self-love. Happiness is a gift, achievement, and a state of mind you can only give yourself. But I have a hint for you. You didn't actually think I was going to bring you all this way and just leave you hanging, did you? Of course not. So here is the hint.

Happiness is love. And it's not the love you receive. Happiness is the love you give. You will find happiness more often when you are giving love. Giving love creates happiness. Giving love also increases your chances of receiving love. However, you do not need to receive love in order to give love. Happiness is a person who can give unconditional love regardless of their circumstances. A person who dies loving, is a person who dies happy. Love is an eternal gift. Happiness is only eternal when connected to love.

So you ask me how to find happiness? The answer is to love. But you can only love when you feel love from inside. I have desperately tried in this book to show you a way to develop a love for yourself. I cannot just wave a magic wand and give it to you. You have to create it for yourself. It is your own journey. I have lit a path for you. I have guided you down that path. But it is up to you to actually walk down the path. You are in control. You are empowered. I hope you choose to walk the path and find your happiness. I wish you nothing but love in doing so. In deciding to walk down that path, you are Rising To Greatness.

ACKNOWLEDGEMENTS

Thank you Sarah Delamere Hurding for your editorial assistance,
encouragement, and endless support.

Made in the USA
San Bernardino, CA
22 July 2020

75828837R10106